MW01106568

Wine Name: _____
Winery: _____
Region: _____
Grapes: _____
Vintage: _____
Alcohol %: _____

KEEP CALM AND DRINK WINE

❋ Aroma ❋

Wine Not?

Primary Aromas: _____

Secondary Aromas: _____

Tertiary Aromas: _____

L♥VE WINE

▬ Finish ▬

○ Soft Finish

○ Tart & Tingly

○ Juicy & Fresh

Tannin

LOW   MED   HIGH

Acidity

LOW   MED   HIGH

Body

LOW   MED   HIGH

★ Rating ★

Appearance	☆☆☆☆☆
Aroma	☆☆☆☆☆
Body	☆☆☆☆☆
Taste	☆☆☆☆☆
Finish	☆☆☆☆☆
Overall Rating	☆☆☆☆☆

Home is where THE WINE IS

Wine Name: _____

Winery: _____

Region: _____

Grapes: _____

Vintage: _____

Alcohol %: _____

AROMA

Primary Aromas: _____

Secondary Aromas: _____

Tertiary Aromas: _____

TANNIN

LOW _____ MED _____ HIGH

ACIDITY

LOW _____ MED _____ HIGH

BODY

LOW _____ MED _____ HIGH

FINISH

○ Soft Finish   ○ Tart & Tingly   ○ Juicy & Fresh

LIFE IS TOO SHORT TO DRINK BAD WINE

WINE A BIT you'll feel better

RATING

Appearance	☆ ☆ ☆ ☆ ☆
Aroma	☆ ☆ ☆ ☆ ☆
Body	☆ ☆ ☆ ☆ ☆
Taste	☆ ☆ ☆ ☆ ☆
Finish	☆ ☆ ☆ ☆ ☆
Overall Rating	☆ ☆ ☆ ☆ ☆

time to
wine down

Wine Name: _____

Winery: _____

Region: _____

Grapes: _____

Vintage: _____

Alcohol %: _____

KEEP CALM AND DRINK WINE

Wine Not?

⁂ Aroma ⁂

Primary Aromas: _____

Secondary Aromas: _____

Tertiary Aromas: _____

L♥VE WINE

◼ Finish ◼

○ Soft Finish

○ Tart & Tingly

○ Juicy & Fresh

Tannin

LOW   MED   HIGH

Acidity

LOW   MED   HIGH

Body

LOW   MED   HIGH

★ Rating ★

Appearance	☆ ☆ ☆ ☆ ☆
Aroma	☆ ☆ ☆ ☆ ☆
Body	☆ ☆ ☆ ☆ ☆
Taste	☆ ☆ ☆ ☆ ☆
Finish	☆ ☆ ☆ ☆ ☆
Overall Rating	☆ ☆ ☆ ☆ ☆

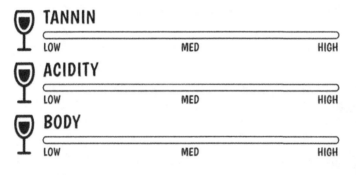

Home is where THE WINE IS

Wine Name: _____

Winery: _____

Region: _____

Grapes: _____

Vintage: _____

Alcohol %: _____

AROMA

Primary Aromas: _____

Secondary Aromas: _____

Tertiary Aromas: _____

TANNIN

LOW   MED   HIGH

ACIDITY

LOW   MED   HIGH

BODY

LOW   MED   HIGH

FINISH

○ Soft Finish   ○ Tart & Tingly   ○ Juicy & Fresh

LIFE IS TOO SHORT TO DRINK BAD WINE

WINE A BIT *you'll feel better*

RATING

Appearance	☆ ☆ ☆ ☆ ☆
Aroma	☆ ☆ ☆ ☆ ☆
Body	☆ ☆ ☆ ☆ ☆
Taste	☆ ☆ ☆ ☆ ☆
Finish	☆ ☆ ☆ ☆ ☆
Overall Rating	☆ ☆ ☆ ☆ ☆

time to wine down

Wine Name: _____

Winery: _____

Region: _____

Grapes: _____

Vintage: _____

Alcohol %: _____

KEEP CALM AND DRINK WINE

Wine Not?

Aroma

Primary Aromas: _____

Secondary Aromas: _____

Tertiary Aromas: _____

LOVE WINE

Finish

- O Soft Finish
- O Tart & Tingly
- O Juicy & Fresh

Tannin

LOW ———————— MED ———————— HIGH

Acidity

LOW ———————— MED ———————— HIGH

Body

LOW ———————— MED ———————— HIGH

Rating

Appearance	☆	☆	☆	☆	☆
Aroma	☆	☆	☆	☆	☆
Body	☆	☆	☆	☆	☆
Taste	☆	☆	☆	☆	☆
Finish	☆	☆	☆	☆	☆
Overall Rating	☆	☆	☆	☆	☆

Home is where THE WINE IS

Wine Name: _____

Winery: _____

Region: _____

Grapes: _____

Vintage: _____

Alcohol %: _____

AROMA

Primary Aromas: _____

Secondary Aromas: _____

Tertiary Aromas: _____

TANNIN
LOW   MED   HIGH

ACIDITY
LOW   MED   HIGH

BODY
LOW   MED   HIGH

LIFE IS TOO SHORT TO DRINK BAD WINE

FINISH

○ Soft Finish   ○ Tart & Tingly   ○ Juicy & Fresh

WINE A BIT you'll feel better

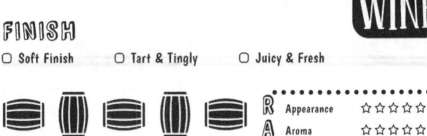

RATING		
Appearance	☆☆☆☆☆
Aroma	☆☆☆☆☆
Body	☆☆☆☆☆
Taste	☆☆☆☆☆
Finish	☆☆☆☆☆
Overall Rating	☆☆☆☆☆

time to wine down

Wine Name: _____

Winery: _____

Region: _____

Grapes: _____

Vintage: _____

Alcohol %: _____

KEEP CALM AND DRINK WINE

Wine Not?

Aroma

Primary Aromas: _____

Secondary Aromas: _____

Tertiary Aromas: _____

LOVE WINE

Finish

- ○ Soft Finish
- ○ Tart & Tingly
- ○ Juicy & Fresh

Tannin

LOW   MED   HIGH

Acidity

LOW   MED   HIGH

Body

LOW   MED   HIGH

Rating

Appearance	☆ ☆ ☆ ☆ ☆
Aroma	☆ ☆ ☆ ☆ ☆
Body	☆ ☆ ☆ ☆ ☆
Taste	☆ ☆ ☆ ☆ ☆
Finish	☆ ☆ ☆ ☆ ☆
Overall Rating	☆ ☆ ☆ ☆ ☆

Wine Name: _____

Winery: _____

Region: _____

Grapes: _____

Vintage: _____

Alcohol %: _____

AROMA

Primary Aromas: _____

Secondary Aromas: _____

Tertiary Aromas: _____

TANNIN
LOW   MED   HIGH

ACIDITY
LOW   MED   HIGH

BODY
LOW   MED   HIGH

FINISH

○ Soft Finish   ○ Tart & Tingly   ○ Juicy & Fresh

RATING		
Appearance	☆☆☆☆☆
Aroma	☆☆☆☆☆
Body	☆☆☆☆☆
Taste	☆☆☆☆☆
Finish	☆☆☆☆☆
Overall Rating	☆☆☆☆☆

time to wine down

Wine Name: _____

Winery: _____

Region: _____

Grapes: _____

Vintage: _____

Alcohol %: _____

KEEP CALM AND DRINK WINE

Wine Not?

Aroma

Primary Aromas: _____

Secondary Aromas: _____

Tertiary Aromas: _____

LOVE WINE

Finish

- ○ Soft Finish
- ○ Tart & Tingly
- ○ Juicy & Fresh

Tannin

LOW   MED   HIGH

Acidity

LOW   MED   HIGH

Body

LOW   MED   HIGH

★ Rating ★

Appearance	☆ ☆ ☆ ☆ ☆
Aroma	☆ ☆ ☆ ☆ ☆
Body	☆ ☆ ☆ ☆ ☆
Taste	☆ ☆ ☆ ☆ ☆
Finish	☆ ☆ ☆ ☆ ☆
Overall Rating	☆ ☆ ☆ ☆ ☆

Home is where ≥THE WINE IS≤

Wine Name: _____

Winery: _____

Region: _____

Grapes: _____

Vintage: _____

Alcohol %: _____

AROMA

Primary Aromas: _____

Secondary Aromas: _____

Tertiary Aromas: _____

TANNIN
LOW   MED   HIGH

ACIDITY
LOW   MED   HIGH

BODY
LOW   MED   HIGH

LIFE IS TOO SHORT TO DRINK BAD WINE

FINISH

○ Soft Finish   ○ Tart & Tingly   ○ Juicy & Fresh

WINE A BIT you'll feel better

RATING

Appearance	☆ ☆ ☆ ☆ ☆
Aroma	☆ ☆ ☆ ☆ ☆
Body	☆ ☆ ☆ ☆ ☆
Taste	☆ ☆ ☆ ☆ ☆
Finish	☆ ☆ ☆ ☆ ☆
Overall Rating	☆ ☆ ☆ ☆ ☆

time to **wine down**

Wine Name: _____

Winery: _____

Region: _____

Grapes: _____

Vintage: _____

Alcohol %: _____

KEEP CALM AND DRINK WINE

Aroma

Primary Aromas: _____

Secondary Aromas: _____

Tertiary Aromas: _____

Wine Not?

LOVE WINE

Finish

- ○ Soft Finish
- ○ Tart & Tingly
- ○ Juicy & Fresh

Tannin

LOW	MED	HIGH

Acidity

LOW	MED	HIGH

Body

LOW	MED	HIGH

★ Rating ★

Appearance	☆☆☆☆☆
Aroma	☆☆☆☆☆
Body	☆☆☆☆☆
Taste	☆☆☆☆☆
Finish	☆☆☆☆☆
Overall Rating	☆☆☆☆☆

Wine Name: _____

Winery: _____

Region: _____

Grapes: _____

Vintage: _____

Alcohol %: _____

AROMA

Primary Aromas: _____

Secondary Aromas: _____

Tertiary Aromas: _____

Home is where THE WINE IS

TANNIN
LOW   MED   HIGH

ACIDITY
LOW   MED   HIGH

BODY
LOW   MED   HIGH

FINISH

○ Soft Finish   ○ Tart & Tingly   ○ Juicy & Fresh

WINE A BIT *you'll feel better*

RATING

Appearance	☆ ☆ ☆ ☆ ☆
Aroma	☆ ☆ ☆ ☆ ☆
Body	☆ ☆ ☆ ☆ ☆
Taste	☆ ☆ ☆ ☆ ☆
Finish	☆ ☆ ☆ ☆ ☆
Overall Rating	☆ ☆ ☆ ☆ ☆

time to
wine down

Wine Name: _____

Winery: _____

Region: _____

Grapes: _____

Vintage: _____

Alcohol %: _____

KEEP CALM AND DRINK WINE

Wine Not?

❧ Aroma ❧

Primary Aromas: _____

Secondary Aromas: _____

Tertiary Aromas: _____

LOVE WINE

Finish

○ Soft Finish
○ Tart & Tingly
○ Juicy & Fresh

Tannin

OW   MED   HIGH

Acidity

OW   MED   HIGH

Body

OW   MED   HIGH

Rating

Appearance	☆ ☆ ☆ ☆ ☆
Aroma	☆ ☆ ☆ ☆ ☆
Body	☆ ☆ ☆ ☆ ☆
Taste	☆ ☆ ☆ ☆ ☆
Finish	☆ ☆ ☆ ☆ ☆
Overall Rating	☆ ☆ ☆ ☆ ☆

Wine Name: _____

Winery: _____

Region: _____

Grapes: _____

Vintage: _____

Alcohol %: _____

Home is where THE WINE IS

AROMA

Primary Aromas: _____

Secondary Aromas: _____

Tertiary Aromas: _____

TANNIN

LOW   MED   HIGH

ACIDITY

LOW   MED   HIGH

BODY

LOW   MED   HIGH

FINISH

○ Soft Finish   ○ Tart & Tingly   ○ Juicy & Fresh

LIFE IS TOO SHORT TO DRINK BAD WINE

WINE A BIT you'll feel better

RATING

Appearance	☆☆☆☆☆
Aroma	☆☆☆☆☆
Body	☆☆☆☆☆
Taste	☆☆☆☆☆
Finish	☆☆☆☆☆
Overall Rating	☆☆☆☆☆

time to
wine down

Wine Name: _____

Winery: _____

Region: _____

Grapes: _____

Vintage: _____

Alcohol %: _____

KEEP CALM AND DRINK WINE

Aroma

Primary Aromas: _____

Secondary Aromas: _____

Tertiary Aromas: _____

Wine Not?

L♥VE WINE

Finish

○ Soft Finish

○ Tart & Tingly

○ Juicy & Fresh

Tannin

LOW	MED	HIGH

Acidity

LOW	MED	HIGH

Body

LOW	MED	HIGH

★ Rating ★

Appearance	☆☆☆☆☆
Aroma	☆☆☆☆☆
Body	☆☆☆☆☆
Taste	☆☆☆☆☆
Finish	☆☆☆☆☆
Overall Rating	☆☆☆☆☆

Home is where =THE WINE IS=

Wine Name: _____

Winery: _____

Region: _____

Grapes: _____

Vintage: _____

Alcohol %: _____

AROMA

Primary Aromas: _____

Secondary Aromas: _____

Tertiary Aromas: _____

TANNIN
LOW   MED   HIGH

ACIDITY
LOW   MED   HIGH

BODY
LOW   MED   HIGH

FINISH

○ Soft Finish   ○ Tart & Tingly   ○ Juicy & Fresh

LIFE IS TOO SHORT TO DRINK BAD WINE

WINE A BIT you'll feel better

RATING		
Appearance	☆☆☆☆☆
Aroma	☆☆☆☆☆
Body	☆☆☆☆☆
Taste	☆☆☆☆☆
Finish	☆☆☆☆☆
Overall Rating	☆☆☆☆☆

time to
wine down

Wine Name: _____

Winery: _____

Region: _____

Grapes: _____

Vintage: _____

Alcohol %: _____

KEEP CALM AND DRINK WINE

Wine Not?

❀ Aroma ❀

Primary Aromas: _____

Secondary Aromas: _____

Tertiary Aromas: _____

L♥VE W♥NE

Finish

○ Soft Finish

○ Tart & Tingly

○ Juicy & Fresh

Tannin

LOW	MED	HIGH

Acidity

LOW	MED	HIGH

Body

LOW	MED	HIGH

★ Rating ★

Appearance	☆ ☆ ☆ ☆ ☆
Aroma	☆ ☆ ☆ ☆ ☆
Body	☆ ☆ ☆ ☆ ☆
Taste	☆ ☆ ☆ ☆ ☆
Finish	☆ ☆ ☆ ☆ ☆
Overall Rating	☆ ☆ ☆ ☆ ☆

Wine Name: _____

Winery: _____

Region: _____

Grapes: _____

Vintage: _____

Alcohol %: _____

AROMA

Primary Aromas: _____

Secondary Aromas: _____

Tertiary Aromas: _____

TANNIN

LOW   MED   HIGH

ACIDITY

LOW   MED   HIGH

BODY

LOW   MED   HIGH

FINISH

○ Soft Finish   ○ Tart & Tingly   ○ Juicy & Fresh

RATING		
Appearance	☆☆☆☆☆
Aroma	☆☆☆☆☆
Body	☆☆☆☆☆
Taste	☆☆☆☆☆
Finish	☆☆☆☆☆
Overall Rating	☆☆☆☆☆

time to
wine down

Wine Name: _____

Winery: _____

Region: _____

Grapes: _____

Vintage: _____

Alcohol %: _____

KEEP CALM AND DRINK WINE

Aroma

Primary Aromas: _____

Secondary Aromas: _____

Tertiary Aromas: _____

Wine Not?

LOVE WINE

Finish

- ○ Soft Finish
- ○ Tart & Tingly
- ○ Juicy & Fresh

Tannin

LOW   MED   HIGH

Acidity

LOW   MED   HIGH

Body

LOW   MED   HIGH

Rating

Appearance	☆☆☆☆☆
Aroma	☆☆☆☆☆
Body	☆☆☆☆☆
Taste	☆☆☆☆☆
Finish	☆☆☆☆☆
Overall Rating	☆☆☆☆☆

Wine Name: _____

Winery: _____

Region: _____

Grapes: _____

Vintage: _____

Alcohol %: _____

Home is where THE WINE IS

AROMA

Primary Aromas: _____

Secondary Aromas: _____

Tertiary Aromas: _____

TANNIN
LOW   MED   HIGH

ACIDITY
LOW   MED   HIGH

BODY
LOW   MED   HIGH

FINISH

○ Soft Finish   ○ Tart & Tingly   ○ Juicy & Fresh

LIFE IS TOO SHORT TO DRINK BAD WINE

WINE A BIT you'll feel better

RATING		
Appearance	☆☆☆☆☆
Aroma	☆☆☆☆☆
Body	☆☆☆☆☆
Taste	☆☆☆☆☆
Finish	☆☆☆☆☆
Overall Rating	☆☆☆☆☆

time to wine down

Wine Name: _____

Winery: _____

Region: _____

Grapes: _____

Vintage: _____

Alcohol %: _____

KEEP CALM AND DRINK WINE

Wine Not?

❦ Aroma ❦

Primary Aromas: _____

Secondary Aromas: _____

Tertiary Aromas: _____

L♥VE WINE

▬ Finish ▬

○ Soft Finish

○ Tart & Tingly

○ Juicy & Fresh

Tannin

LOW   MED   HIGH

Acidity

LOW   MED   HIGH

Body

LOW   MED   HIGH

★ Rating ★

Appearance	☆ ☆ ☆ ☆ ☆
Aroma	☆ ☆ ☆ ☆ ☆
Body	☆ ☆ ☆ ☆ ☆
Taste	☆ ☆ ☆ ☆ ☆
Finish	☆ ☆ ☆ ☆ ☆
Overall Rating	☆ ☆ ☆ ☆ ☆

Wine Name: _____

Winery: _____

Region: _____

Grapes: _____

Vintage: _____

Alcohol %: _____

AROMA

Primary Aromas: _____

Secondary Aromas: _____

Tertiary Aromas: _____

LIFE IS TOO SHORT TO DRINK BAD WINE

TANNIN

LOW   MED   HIGH

ACIDITY

LOW   MED   HIGH

BODY

LOW   MED   HIGH

FINISH

○ Soft Finish   ○ Tart & Tingly   ○ Juicy & Fresh

WINE A BIT you'll feel better

RATING

Appearance	☆ ☆ ☆ ☆ ☆
Aroma	☆ ☆ ☆ ☆ ☆
Body	☆ ☆ ☆ ☆ ☆
Taste	☆ ☆ ☆ ☆ ☆
Finish	☆ ☆ ☆ ☆ ☆
Overall Rating	☆ ☆ ☆ ☆ ☆

time to
wine down

Wine Name: _____

Winery: _____

Region: _____

Grapes: _____

Vintage: _____

Alcohol %: _____

KEEP CALM AND DRINK WINE

✿ Aroma ✿

Wine Not?

Primary Aromas: _____

Secondary Aromas: _____

Tertiary Aromas: _____

LOVE WINE

Finish
- O Soft Finish
- O Tart & Tingly
- O Juicy & Fresh

Tannin

LOW   MED   HIGH

Acidity

LOW   MED   HIGH

Body

LOW   MED   HIGH

★ Rating ★

Appearance	☆☆☆☆☆
Aroma	☆☆☆☆☆
Body	☆☆☆☆☆
Taste	☆☆☆☆☆
Finish	☆☆☆☆☆
Overall Rating	☆☆☆☆☆

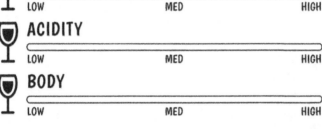

Wine Name: _____

Winery: _____

Region: _____

Grapes: _____

Vintage: _____

Alcohol %: _____

AROMA

Primary Aromas: _____

Secondary Aromas: _____

Tertiary Aromas: _____

TANNIN

LOW   MED   HIGH

ACIDITY

LOW   MED   HIGH

BODY

LOW   MED   HIGH

LIFE IS TOO SHORT TO DRINK BAD WINE

FINISH

○ Soft Finish   ○ Tart & Tingly   ○ Juicy & Fresh

WINE A BIT you'll feel better

RATING

Appearance	☆☆☆☆☆
Aroma	☆☆☆☆☆
Body	☆☆☆☆☆
Taste	☆☆☆☆☆
Finish	☆☆☆☆☆
Overall Rating	☆☆☆☆☆

time to **wine down**

Wine Name: _____

Winery: _____

Region: _____

Grapes: _____

Vintage: _____

Alcohol %: _____

KEEP CALM AND DRINK WINE

⁂ *Aroma* ⁂

Wine Not?

Primary Aromas: _____

Secondary Aromas: _____

Tertiary Aromas: _____

L♥VE W♥NE

▬ *Finish* ▬

○ Soft Finish

○ Tart & Tingly

○ Juicy & Fresh

Tannin

OW   MED   HIGH

Acidity

OW   MED   HIGH

Body

OW   MED   HIGH

★ *Rating* ★

Appearance	☆ ☆ ☆ ☆ ☆
Aroma	☆ ☆ ☆ ☆ ☆
Body	☆ ☆ ☆ ☆ ☆
Taste	☆ ☆ ☆ ☆ ☆
Finish	☆ ☆ ☆ ☆ ☆
Overall Rating	☆ ☆ ☆ ☆ ☆

Home is where
THE WINE IS

Wine Name: _____
Winery: _____
Region: _____
Grapes: _____
Vintage: _____
Alcohol %: _____

AROMA

Primary Aromas: _____
Secondary Aromas: _____
Tertiary Aromas: _____

TANNIN
LOW   MED   HIGH

ACIDITY
LOW   MED   HIGH

BODY
LOW   MED   HIGH

FINISH

○ Soft Finish   ○ Tart & Tingly   ○ Juicy & Fresh

LIFE IS TOO SHORT TO DRINK BAD WINE

WINE A BIT
you'll feel better

RATING

Appearance	☆ ☆ ☆ ☆ ☆
Aroma	☆ ☆ ☆ ☆ ☆
Body	☆ ☆ ☆ ☆ ☆
Taste	☆ ☆ ☆ ☆ ☆
Finish	☆ ☆ ☆ ☆ ☆
Overall Rating	☆ ☆ ☆ ☆ ☆

time to wine down

Wine Name: _____

Winery: _____

Region: _____

Grapes: _____

Vintage: _____

Alcohol %: _____

KEEP CALM AND DRINK WINE

Aroma

Wine Not!?

Primary Aromas: _____

Secondary Aromas: _____

Tertiary Aromas: _____

LOVE WINE

Finish

- ☐ Soft Finish
- ☐ Tart & Tingly
- ☐ Juicy & Fresh

Tannin

LOW   MED   HIGH

Acidity

LOW   MED   HIGH

Body

LOW   MED   HIGH

Rating

Appearance	☆☆☆☆☆
Aroma	☆☆☆☆☆
Body	☆☆☆☆☆
Taste	☆☆☆☆☆
Finish	☆☆☆☆☆
Overall Rating	☆☆☆☆☆

Wine Name: _____

Winery: _____

Region: _____

Grapes: _____

Vintage: _____

Alcohol %: _____

Home is where =THE WINE IS=

AROMA

Primary Aromas: _____

Secondary Aromas: _____

Tertiary Aromas: _____

TANNIN

LOW　　　　MED　　　　HIGH

ACIDITY

LOW　　　　MED　　　　HIGH

BODY

LOW　　　　MED　　　　HIGH

FINISH

○ Soft Finish　　○ Tart & Tingly　　○ Juicy & Fresh

LIFE IS TOO SHORT TO DRINK BAD WINE

WINE A BIT you'll feel better

RATING

Appearance	☆☆☆☆☆
Aroma	☆☆☆☆☆
Body	☆☆☆☆☆
Taste	☆☆☆☆☆
Finish	☆☆☆☆☆
Overall Rating	☆☆☆☆☆

time to wine down

Wine Name: _____

Winery: _____

Region: _____

Grapes: _____

Vintage: _____

Alcohol %: _____

KEEP CALM AND DRINK WINE

Aroma

Primary Aromas: _____

Secondary Aromas: _____

Tertiary Aromas: _____

Wine Not?

LOVE WINE

Finish

- ○ Soft Finish
- ○ Tart & Tingly
- ○ Juicy & Fresh

Tannin

LOW   MED   HIGH

Acidity

LOW   MED   HIGH

Body

LOW   MED   HIGH

Rating

Appearance	☆ ☆ ☆ ☆ ☆
Aroma	☆ ☆ ☆ ☆ ☆
Body	☆ ☆ ☆ ☆ ☆
Taste	☆ ☆ ☆ ☆ ☆
Finish	☆ ☆ ☆ ☆ ☆
Overall Rating	☆ ☆ ☆ ☆ ☆

Home is where THE WINE IS

Wine Name: _____

Winery: _____

Region: _____

Grapes: _____

Vintage: _____

Alcohol %: _____

AROMA

Primary Aromas: _____

Secondary Aromas: _____

Tertiary Aromas: _____

TANNIN
LOW   MED   HIGH

ACIDITY
LOW   MED   HIGH

BODY
LOW   MED   HIGH

LIFE IS TOO SHORT TO DRINK BAD WINE

FINISH

○ Soft Finish   ○ Tart & Tingly   ○ Juicy & Fresh

WINE A BIT you'll feel better

RATING

Appearance	☆ ☆ ☆ ☆ ☆
Aroma	☆ ☆ ☆ ☆ ☆
Body	☆ ☆ ☆ ☆ ☆
Taste	☆ ☆ ☆ ☆ ☆
Finish	☆ ☆ ☆ ☆ ☆
Overall Rating	☆ ☆ ☆ ☆ ☆

time to
wine down

Wine Name: _____

Winery: _____

Region: _____

Grapes: _____

Vintage: _____

Alcohol %: _____

KEEP CALM AND DRINK WINE

Wine Not?

✦ Aroma ✦

Primary Aromas: _____

Secondary Aromas: _____

Tertiary Aromas: _____

L♥VE WINE

▬ Finish ▬

- ○ Soft Finish
- ○ Tart & Tingly
- ○ Juicy & Fresh

Tannin

LOW   MED   HIGH

Acidity

LOW   MED   HIGH

Body

LOW   MED   HIGH

★ Rating ★

Appearance	☆☆☆☆☆
Aroma	☆☆☆☆☆
Body	☆☆☆☆☆
Taste	☆☆☆☆☆
Finish	☆☆☆☆☆
Overall Rating	☆☆☆☆☆

Home is where THE WINE IS

Wine Name: _____

Winery: _____

Region: _____

Grapes: _____

Vintage: _____

Alcohol %: _____

AROMA

Primary Aromas: _____

Secondary Aromas: _____

Tertiary Aromas: _____

TANNIN
| LOW | MED | HIGH |

ACIDITY
| LOW | MED | HIGH |

BODY
| LOW | MED | HIGH |

FINISH

○ Soft Finish   ○ Tart & Tingly   ○ Juicy & Fresh

LIFE IS TOO SHORT TO DRINK BAD WINE

WINE A BIT you'll feel better

RATING

Appearance	☆ ☆ ☆ ☆ ☆
Aroma	☆ ☆ ☆ ☆ ☆
Body	☆ ☆ ☆ ☆ ☆
Taste	☆ ☆ ☆ ☆ ☆
Finish	☆ ☆ ☆ ☆ ☆
Overall Rating	☆ ☆ ☆ ☆ ☆

time to
wine down

Wine Name: _____

Winery: _____

Region: _____

Grapes: _____

Vintage: _____

Alcohol %: _____

KEEP CALM AND DRINK WINE

Wine Not?

❖ Aroma ❖

Primary Aromas: _____

Secondary Aromas: _____

Tertiary Aromas: _____

LOVE WINE

▬ Finish ▬

○ Soft Finish

○ Tart & Tingly

○ Juicy & Fresh

Tannin

| LOW | MED | HIGH |

Acidity

| LOW | MED | HIGH |

Body

| LOW | MED | HIGH |

★ Rating ★

Appearance	☆ ☆ ☆ ☆ ☆
Aroma	☆ ☆ ☆ ☆ ☆
Body	☆ ☆ ☆ ☆ ☆
Taste	☆ ☆ ☆ ☆ ☆
Finish	☆ ☆ ☆ ☆ ☆
Overall Rating	☆ ☆ ☆ ☆ ☆

Wine Name: _____

Winery: _____

Region: _____

Grapes: _____

Vintage: _____

Alcohol %: _____

AROMA

Primary Aromas: _____

Secondary Aromas: _____

Tertiary Aromas: _____

TANNIN

LOW   MED   HIGH

ACIDITY

LOW   MED   HIGH

BODY

LOW   MED   HIGH

LIFE IS TOO SHORT TO DRINK BAD WINE

FINISH

○ Soft Finish   ○ Tart & Tingly   ○ Juicy & Fresh

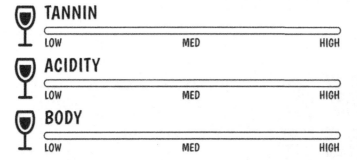

WINE A BIT you'll feel better

RATING		
Appearance	☆☆☆☆☆
Aroma	☆☆☆☆☆
Body	☆☆☆☆☆
Taste	☆☆☆☆☆
Finish	☆☆☆☆☆
Overall Rating	☆☆☆☆☆

time to wine down

Wine Name: _____

Winery: _____

Region: _____

Grapes: _____

Vintage: _____

Alcohol %: _____

KEEP CALM AND DRINK WINE

Wine Not?

Aroma

Primary Aromas: _____

Secondary Aromas: _____

Tertiary Aromas: _____

LOVE WINE

Finish

- ○ Soft Finish
- ○ Tart & Tingly
- ○ Juicy & Fresh

Tannin

LOW   MED   HIGH

Acidity

LOW   MED   HIGH

Body

LOW   MED   HIGH

Rating

Appearance	☆ ☆ ☆ ☆ ☆
Aroma	☆ ☆ ☆ ☆ ☆
Body	☆ ☆ ☆ ☆ ☆
Taste	☆ ☆ ☆ ☆ ☆
Finish	☆ ☆ ☆ ☆ ☆
Overall Rating	☆ ☆ ☆ ☆ ☆

Home is where THE WINE IS

Wine Name: _____
Winery: _____
Region: _____
Grapes: _____
Vintage: _____
Alcohol %: _____

AROMA

Primary Aromas: _____
Secondary Aromas: _____
Tertiary Aromas: _____

TANNIN
LOW   MED   HIGH

ACIDITY
LOW   MED   HIGH

BODY
LOW   MED   HIGH

FINISH

○ Soft Finish   ○ Tart & Tingly   ○ Juicy & Fresh

LIFE IS TOO SHORT TO DRINK BAD WINE

WINE A BIT you'll feel better

RATING		
Appearance	☆☆☆☆☆
Aroma	☆☆☆☆☆
Body	☆☆☆☆☆
Taste	☆☆☆☆☆
Finish	☆☆☆☆☆
Overall Rating	☆☆☆☆☆

time to
wine down

Wine Name: _____

Winery: _____

Region: _____

Grapes: _____

Vintage: _____

Alcohol %: _____

KEEP CALM AND DRINK WINE

✿ Aroma ✿

Wine Not?

Primary Aromas: _____

Secondary Aromas: _____

Tertiary Aromas: _____

LOVE WINE

► Finish ◄

○ Soft Finish

○ Tart & Tingly

○ Juicy & Fresh

Tannin

LOW   MED   HIGH

Acidity

LOW   MED   HIGH

Body

LOW   MED   HIGH

★ Rating ★

Appearance	☆☆☆☆☆
Aroma	☆☆☆☆☆
Body	☆☆☆☆☆
Taste	☆☆☆☆☆
Finish	☆☆☆☆☆
Overall Rating	☆☆☆☆☆

Wine Name: _____

Winery: _____

Region: _____

Grapes: _____

Vintage: _____

Alcohol %: _____

AROMA

Primary Aromas: _____

Secondary Aromas: _____

Tertiary Aromas: _____

TANNIN
LOW   MED   HIGH

ACIDITY
LOW   MED   HIGH

BODY
LOW   MED   HIGH

FINISH

○ Soft Finish   ○ Tart & Tingly   ○ Juicy & Fresh

RATING

Appearance	☆☆☆☆☆
Aroma	☆☆☆☆☆
Body	☆☆☆☆☆
Taste	☆☆☆☆☆
Finish	☆☆☆☆☆
Overall Rating	☆☆☆☆☆

time to wine down

Wine Name: _____

Winery: _____

Region: _____

Grapes: _____

Vintage: _____

Alcohol %: _____

KEEP CALM AND DRINK WINE

Wine Not?

Aroma

Primary Aromas: _____

Secondary Aromas: _____

Tertiary Aromas: _____

LOVE WINE

Finish

- ○ Soft Finish
- ○ Tart & Tingly
- ○ Juicy & Fresh

Tannin

LOW   MED   HIGH

Acidity

LOW   MED   HIGH

Body

LOW   MED   HIGH

★ Rating ★

Appearance	☆ ☆ ☆ ☆ ☆
Aroma	☆ ☆ ☆ ☆ ☆
Body	☆ ☆ ☆ ☆ ☆
Taste	☆ ☆ ☆ ☆ ☆
Finish	☆ ☆ ☆ ☆ ☆
Overall Rating	☆ ☆ ☆ ☆ ☆

Home is where =THE WINE IS=

Wine Name: _____

Winery: _____

Region: _____

Grapes: _____

Vintage: _____

Alcohol %: _____

AROMA

Primary Aromas: _____

Secondary Aromas: _____

Tertiary Aromas: _____

LIFE IS TOO SHORT TO DRINK BAD WINE

TANNIN
LOW   MED   HIGH

ACIDITY
LOW   MED   HIGH

BODY
LOW   MED   HIGH

FINISH

○ Soft Finish   ○ Tart & Tingly   ○ Juicy & Fresh

WINE A BIT you'll feel better

RATING

Appearance	☆ ☆ ☆ ☆ ☆
Aroma	☆ ☆ ☆ ☆ ☆
Body	☆ ☆ ☆ ☆ ☆
Taste	☆ ☆ ☆ ☆ ☆
Finish	☆ ☆ ☆ ☆ ☆
Overall Rating	☆ ☆ ☆ ☆ ☆

time to wine down

Wine Name: _____

Winery: _____

Region: _____

Grapes: _____

Vintage: _____

Alcohol %: _____

KEEP CALM AND DRINK WINE

Wine Not?

Aroma

Primary Aromas: _____

Secondary Aromas: _____

Tertiary Aromas: _____

LOVE WINE

Finish

○ Soft Finish

○ Tart & Tingly

○ Juicy & Fresh

Tannin

LOW   MED   HIGH

Acidity

LOW   MED   HIGH

Body

LOW   MED   HIGH

Rating

Appearance	☆☆☆☆☆
Aroma	☆☆☆☆☆
Body	☆☆☆☆☆
Taste	☆☆☆☆☆
Finish	☆☆☆☆☆
Overall Rating	☆☆☆☆☆

Home is where
=THE WINE IS=

Wine Name: _____

Winery: _____

Region: _____

Grapes: _____

Vintage: _____

Alcohol %: _____

AROMA

Primary Aromas: _____

Secondary Aromas: _____

Tertiary Aromas: _____

TANNIN
LOW   MED   HIGH

ACIDITY
LOW   MED   HIGH

BODY
LOW   MED   HIGH

FINISH

○ Soft Finish   ○ Tart & Tingly   ○ Juicy & Fresh

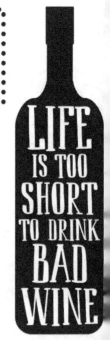

LIFE IS TOO SHORT TO DRINK BAD WINE

WINE A BIT
you'll feel better

RATING

Appearance	☆ ☆ ☆ ☆ ☆
Aroma	☆ ☆ ☆ ☆ ☆
Body	☆ ☆ ☆ ☆ ☆
Taste	☆ ☆ ☆ ☆ ☆
Finish	☆ ☆ ☆ ☆ ☆
Overall Rating	☆ ☆ ☆ ☆ ☆

time to
wine down

Wine Name: _____

Winery: _____

Region: _____

Grapes: _____

Vintage: _____

Alcohol %: _____

KEEP CALM AND DRINK WINE

Wine Not?

❧ Aroma ❧

Primary Aromas: _____

Secondary Aromas: _____

Tertiary Aromas: _____

LOVE WINE

▶ Finish ◀

○ Soft Finish

○ Tart & Tingly

○ Juicy & Fresh

Tannin

OW   MED   HIGH

Acidity

OW   MED   HIGH

Body

OW   MED   HIGH

★ Rating ★

Appearance	☆ ☆ ☆ ☆ ☆
Aroma	☆ ☆ ☆ ☆ ☆
Body	☆ ☆ ☆ ☆ ☆
Taste	☆ ☆ ☆ ☆ ☆
Finish	☆ ☆ ☆ ☆ ☆
Overall Rating	☆ ☆ ☆ ☆ ☆

Home is where THE WINE IS

Wine Name: _____

Winery: _____

Region: _____

Grapes: _____

Vintage: _____

Alcohol %: _____

AROMA

Primary Aromas: _____

Secondary Aromas: _____

Tertiary Aromas: _____

TANNIN

LOW   MED   HIGH

ACIDITY

LOW   MED   HIGH

BODY

LOW   MED   HIGH

LIFE IS TOO SHORT TO DRINK BAD WINE

FINISH

○ Soft Finish   ○ Tart & Tingly   ○ Juicy & Fresh

WINE A BIT you'll feel better

RATING

Appearance	☆ ☆ ☆ ☆ ☆
Aroma	☆ ☆ ☆ ☆ ☆
Body	☆ ☆ ☆ ☆ ☆
Taste	☆ ☆ ☆ ☆ ☆
Finish	☆ ☆ ☆ ☆ ☆
Overall Rating	☆ ☆ ☆ ☆ ☆

time to wine down

Wine Name: _____

Winery: _____

Region: _____

Grapes: _____

Vintage: _____

Alcohol %: _____

KEEP CALM AND DRINK WINE

Aroma

Primary Aromas: _____

Secondary Aromas: _____

Tertiary Aromas: _____

Wine Not?

LOVE WINE

Finish

○ Soft Finish

○ Tart & Tingly

○ Juicy & Fresh

Tannin
LOW   MED   HIGH

Acidity
LOW   MED   HIGH

Body
LOW   MED   HIGH

★ Rating ★

Appearance	☆☆☆☆☆
Aroma	☆☆☆☆☆
Body	☆☆☆☆☆
Taste	☆☆☆☆☆
Finish	☆☆☆☆☆
Overall Rating	☆☆☆☆☆

Home is where THE WINE IS

Wine Name: _____

Winery: _____

Region: _____

Grapes: _____

Vintage: _____

Alcohol %: _____

AROMA

Primary Aromas: _____

Secondary Aromas: _____

Tertiary Aromas: _____

TANNIN
LOW   MED   HIGH

ACIDITY
LOW   MED   HIGH

BODY
LOW   MED   HIGH

FINISH

○ Soft Finish   ○ Tart & Tingly   ○ Juicy & Fresh

LIFE IS TOO SHORT TO DRINK BAD WINE

WINE A BIT
you'll feel better

RATING

Appearance	☆☆☆☆☆
Aroma	☆☆☆☆☆
Body	☆☆☆☆☆
Taste	☆☆☆☆☆
Finish	☆☆☆☆☆
Overall Rating	☆☆☆☆☆

time to wine down

Wine Name: _____

Winery: _____

Region: _____

Grapes: _____

Vintage: _____

Alcohol %: _____

KEEP CALM AND DRINK WINE

Wine Not?

Aroma

Primary Aromas: _____

Secondary Aromas: _____

Tertiary Aromas: _____

LOVE WINE

Finish

- ☐ Soft Finish
- ☐ Tart & Tingly
- ☐ Juicy & Fresh

Tannin

LOW — MED — HIGH

Acidity

LOW — MED — HIGH

Body

LOW — MED — HIGH

★ Rating ★

Appearance	☆☆☆☆☆
Aroma	☆☆☆☆☆
Body	☆☆☆☆☆
Taste	☆☆☆☆☆
Finish	☆☆☆☆☆
Overall Rating	☆☆☆☆☆

Wine Name: _____

Winery: _____

Region: _____

Grapes: _____

Vintage: _____

Alcohol %: _____

Home is where THE WINE IS

AROMA

Primary Aromas: _____

Secondary Aromas: _____

Tertiary Aromas: _____

TANNIN
LOW   MED   HIGH

ACIDITY
LOW   MED   HIGH

BODY
LOW   MED   HIGH

FINISH

○ Soft Finish   ○ Tart & Tingly   ○ Juicy & Fresh

WINE A BIT
you'll feel better

RATING

Appearance	☆ ☆ ☆ ☆ ☆
Aroma	☆ ☆ ☆ ☆ ☆
Body	☆ ☆ ☆ ☆ ☆
Taste	☆ ☆ ☆ ☆ ☆
Finish	☆ ☆ ☆ ☆ ☆
Overall Rating	☆ ☆ ☆ ☆ ☆

time to wine down

Wine Name: _____

Winery: _____

Region: _____

Grapes: _____

Vintage: _____

Alcohol %: _____

KEEP CALM AND DRINK WINE

Wine Not?

✦ Aroma ✦

Primary Aromas: _____

Secondary Aromas: _____

Tertiary Aromas: _____

L♥VE W♥NE

▬ Finish ▬

- ○ Soft Finish
- ○ Tart & Tingly
- ○ Juicy & Fresh

Tannin

OW   MED   HIGH

Acidity

OW   MED   HIGH

Body

OW   MED   HIGH

★ Rating ★

Appearance	☆☆☆☆☆
Aroma	☆☆☆☆☆
Body	☆☆☆☆☆
Taste	☆☆☆☆☆
Finish	☆☆☆☆☆
Overall Rating	☆☆☆☆☆

Home is where =THE WINE IS=

Wine Name: _____

Winery: _____

Region: _____

Grapes: _____

Vintage: _____

Alcohol %: _____

AROMA

Primary Aromas: _____

Secondary Aromas: _____

Tertiary Aromas: _____

TANNIN

LOW   MED   HIGH

ACIDITY

LOW   MED   HIGH

BODY

LOW   MED   HIGH

LIFE IS TOO SHORT TO DRINK BAD WINE

FINISH

○ Soft Finish   ○ Tart & Tingly   ○ Juicy & Fresh

WINE A BIT you'll feel better

RATING

Appearance	☆ ☆ ☆ ☆ ☆
Aroma	☆ ☆ ☆ ☆ ☆
Body	☆ ☆ ☆ ☆ ☆
Taste	☆ ☆ ☆ ☆ ☆
Finish	☆ ☆ ☆ ☆ ☆
Overall Rating	☆ ☆ ☆ ☆ ☆

time to wine down

Wine Name: _____

Winery: _____

Region: _____

Grapes: _____

Vintage: _____

Alcohol %: _____

KEEP CALM AND DRINK WINE

Wine Not?

Aroma

Primary Aromas: _____

Secondary Aromas: _____

Tertiary Aromas: _____

LOVE WINE

Finish

○ Soft Finish

○ Tart & Tingly

○ Juicy & Fresh

Tannin

LOW — MED — HIGH

Acidity

LOW — MED — HIGH

Body

LOW — MED — HIGH

Rating

Appearance	☆☆☆☆☆
Aroma	☆☆☆☆☆
Body	☆☆☆☆☆
Taste	☆☆☆☆☆
Finish	☆☆☆☆☆
Overall Rating	☆☆☆☆☆

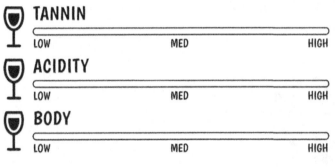

Home is where =THE WINE IS=

Wine Name: _____

Winery: _____

Region: _____

Grapes: _____

Vintage: _____

Alcohol %: _____

AROMA

Primary Aromas: _____

Secondary Aromas: _____

Tertiary Aromas: _____

TANNIN
LOW   MED   HIGH

ACIDITY
LOW   MED   HIGH

BODY
LOW   MED   HIGH

FINISH

○ Soft Finish   ○ Tart & Tingly   ○ Juicy & Fresh

LIFE IS TOO SHORT TO DRINK BAD WINE

WINE A BIT
you'll feel better

RATING

Appearance	☆ ☆ ☆ ☆ ☆
Aroma	☆ ☆ ☆ ☆ ☆
Body	☆ ☆ ☆ ☆ ☆
Taste	☆ ☆ ☆ ☆ ☆
Finish	☆ ☆ ☆ ☆ ☆
Overall Rating	☆ ☆ ☆ ☆ ☆

time to wine down

Wine Name: _____

Winery: _____

Region: _____

Grapes: _____

Vintage: _____

Alcohol %: _____

KEEP CALM AND DRINK WINE

Wine Not?

Aroma

Primary Aromas: _____

Secondary Aromas: _____

Tertiary Aromas: _____

LOVE WINE

Finish

○ Soft Finish

○ Tart & Tingly

○ Juicy & Fresh

Tannin

LOW   MED   HIGH

Acidity

LOW   MED   HIGH

Body

LOW   MED   HIGH

Rating

Appearance	☆ ☆ ☆ ☆ ☆
Aroma	☆ ☆ ☆ ☆ ☆
Body	☆ ☆ ☆ ☆ ☆
Taste	☆ ☆ ☆ ☆ ☆
Finish	☆ ☆ ☆ ☆ ☆
Overall Rating	☆ ☆ ☆ ☆ ☆

Wine Name: _____

Winery: _____

Region: _____

Grapes: _____

Vintage: _____

Alcohol %: _____

Home is where THE WINE IS

AROMA

Primary Aromas: _____

Secondary Aromas: _____

Tertiary Aromas: _____

TANNIN

LOW   MED   HIGH

ACIDITY

LOW   MED   HIGH

BODY

LOW   MED   HIGH

FINISH

○ Soft Finish   ○ Tart & Tingly   ○ Juicy & Fresh

LIFE IS TOO SHORT TO DRINK BAD WINE

WINE A BIT you'll feel better

RATING

Appearance	☆☆☆☆☆
Aroma	☆☆☆☆☆
Body	☆☆☆☆☆
Taste	☆☆☆☆☆
Finish	☆☆☆☆☆
Overall Rating	☆☆☆☆☆

time to
wine down

Wine Name: _____

Winery: _____

Region: _____

Grapes: _____

Vintage: _____

Alcohol %: _____

KEEP CALM AND DRINK WINE

Aroma

Primary Aromas: _____

Secondary Aromas: _____

Tertiary Aromas: _____

Wine Not?

L♥VE WINE

Finish

O Soft Finish

O Tart & Tingly

O Juicy & Fresh

Tannin

OW   MED   HIGH

Acidity

OW   MED   HIGH

Body

OW   MED   HIGH

★ **Rating** ★

Appearance	☆☆☆☆☆
Aroma	☆☆☆☆☆
Body	☆☆☆☆☆
Taste	☆☆☆☆☆
Finish	☆☆☆☆☆
Overall Rating	☆☆☆☆☆

Home is where THE WINE IS

Wine Name: _____
Winery: _____
Region: _____
Grapes: _____
Vintage: _____
Alcohol %: _____

AROMA

Primary Aromas: _____
Secondary Aromas: _____
Tertiary Aromas: _____

TANNIN
LOW   MED   HIGH

ACIDITY
LOW   MED   HIGH

BODY
LOW   MED   HIGH

LIFE IS TOO SHORT TO DRINK BAD WINE

FINISH

○ Soft Finish   ○ Tart & Tingly   ○ Juicy & Fresh

WINE A BIT you'll feel better

RATING

Appearance	☆☆☆☆☆
Aroma	☆☆☆☆☆
Body	☆☆☆☆☆
Taste	☆☆☆☆☆
Finish	☆☆☆☆☆
Overall Rating	☆☆☆☆☆

time to wine down

Wine Name: _____

Winery: _____

Region: _____

Grapes: _____

Vintage: _____

Alcohol %: _____

KEEP CALM AND DRINK WINE

Wine Not?

Aroma

Primary Aromas: _____

Secondary Aromas: _____

Tertiary Aromas: _____

LOVE WINE

Finish

- O Soft Finish
- O Tart & Tingly
- O Juicy & Fresh

Tannin

LOW   MED   HIGH

Acidity

LOW   MED   HIGH

Body

LOW   MED   HIGH

Rating

Appearance	☆ ☆ ☆ ☆ ☆
Aroma	☆ ☆ ☆ ☆ ☆
Body	☆ ☆ ☆ ☆ ☆
Taste	☆ ☆ ☆ ☆ ☆
Finish	☆ ☆ ☆ ☆ ☆
Overall Rating	☆ ☆ ☆ ☆ ☆

Home is where THE WINE IS

Wine Name: _____

Winery: _____

Region: _____

Grapes: _____

Vintage: _____

Alcohol %: _____

AROMA

Primary Aromas: _____

Secondary Aromas: _____

Tertiary Aromas: _____

TANNIN

LOW   MED   HIGH

ACIDITY

LOW   MED   HIGH

BODY

LOW   MED   HIGH

FINISH

○ Soft Finish   ○ Tart & Tingly   ○ Juicy & Fresh

LIFE IS TOO SHORT TO DRINK BAD WINE

WINE A BIT you'll feel better

RATING

Appearance	☆ ☆ ☆ ☆ ☆
Aroma	☆ ☆ ☆ ☆ ☆
Body	☆ ☆ ☆ ☆ ☆
Taste	☆ ☆ ☆ ☆ ☆
Finish	☆ ☆ ☆ ☆ ☆
Overall Rating	☆ ☆ ☆ ☆ ☆

time to
wine down

Wine Name: _____

Winery: _____

Region: _____

Grapes: _____

Vintage: _____

Alcohol %: _____

KEEP CALM AND DRINK WINE

Wine Not?

✾ Aroma ✾

Primary Aromas: _____

Secondary Aromas: _____

Tertiary Aromas: _____

L♥VE WINE

▶ Finish ◀

○ Soft Finish

○ Tart & Tingly

○ Juicy & Fresh

Tannin

LOW	MED	HIGH

Acidity

LOW	MED	HIGH

Body

LOW	MED	HIGH

★ Rating ★

Appearance	☆☆☆☆☆
Aroma	☆☆☆☆☆
Body	☆☆☆☆☆
Taste	☆☆☆☆☆
Finish	☆☆☆☆☆
Overall Rating	☆☆☆☆☆

Wine Name: _____

Winery: _____

Region: _____

Grapes: _____

Vintage: _____

Alcohol %: _____

AROMA

Primary Aromas: _____

Secondary Aromas: _____

Tertiary Aromas: _____

TANNIN

LOW   MED   HIGH

ACIDITY

LOW   MED   HIGH

BODY

LOW   MED   HIGH

FINISH

○ Soft Finish   ○ Tart & Tingly   ○ Juicy & Fresh

Home is where THE WINE IS

LIFE IS TOO SHORT TO DRINK BAD WINE

WINE A BIT *you'll feel better*

RATING		
Appearance	☆☆☆☆☆
Aroma	☆☆☆☆☆
Body	☆☆☆☆☆
Taste	☆☆☆☆☆
Finish	☆☆☆☆☆
Overall Rating	☆☆☆☆☆

time to wine down

Wine Name: _____

Winery: _____

Region: _____

Grapes: _____

Vintage: _____

Alcohol %: _____

KEEP CALM AND DRINK WINE

Wine Not?

Aroma

Primary Aromas: _____

Secondary Aromas: _____

Tertiary Aromas: _____

LOVE WINE

Finish
- ○ Soft Finish
- ○ Tart & Tingly
- ○ Juicy & Fresh

Tannin

LOW	MED	HIGH

Acidity

LOW	MED	HIGH

Body

LOW	MED	HIGH

★ Rating ★

Appearance	☆ ☆ ☆ ☆ ☆
Aroma	☆ ☆ ☆ ☆ ☆
Body	☆ ☆ ☆ ☆ ☆
Taste	☆ ☆ ☆ ☆ ☆
Finish	☆ ☆ ☆ ☆ ☆
Overall Rating	☆ ☆ ☆ ☆ ☆

Wine Name: _____

Winery: _____

Region: _____

Grapes: _____

Vintage: _____

Alcohol %: _____

Home is where THE WINE IS

: AROMA

Primary Aromas: _____

Secondary Aromas: _____

Tertiary Aromas: _____

TANNIN

LOW   MED   HIGH

ACIDITY

LOW   MED   HIGH

BODY

LOW   MED   HIGH

LIFE IS TOO SHORT TO DRINK BAD WINE

FINISH

○ Soft Finish   ○ Tart & Tingly   ○ Juicy & Fresh

WINE A BIT you'll feel better

RATING

Appearance	☆☆☆☆☆
Aroma	☆☆☆☆☆
Body	☆☆☆☆☆
Taste	☆☆☆☆☆
Finish	☆☆☆☆☆
Overall Rating	☆☆☆☆☆

time to wine down

Wine Name: _____

Winery: _____

Region: _____

Grapes: _____

Vintage: _____

Alcohol %: _____

KEEP CALM AND DRINK WINE

Wine Not?

※ Aroma ※

Primary Aromas: _____

Secondary Aromas: _____

Tertiary Aromas: _____

L♥VE WINE

▬ Finish ▬

○ Soft Finish

○ Tart & Tingly

○ Juicy & Fresh

Tannin

| LOW | MED | HIGH |

Acidity

| LOW | MED | HIGH |

Body

| LOW | MED | HIGH |

★ Rating ★

Appearance	☆ ☆ ☆ ☆ ☆
Aroma	☆ ☆ ☆ ☆ ☆
Body	☆ ☆ ☆ ☆ ☆
Taste	☆ ☆ ☆ ☆ ☆
Finish	☆ ☆ ☆ ☆ ☆
Overall Rating	☆ ☆ ☆ ☆ ☆

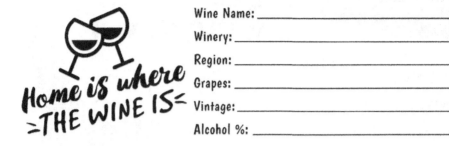

Home is where =THE WINE IS=

Wine Name: _____

Winery: _____

Region: _____

Grapes: _____

Vintage: _____

Alcohol %: _____

AROMA

Primary Aromas: _____

Secondary Aromas: _____

Tertiary Aromas: _____

TANNIN

LOW   MED   HIGH

ACIDITY

LOW   MED   HIGH

BODY

LOW   MED   HIGH

FINISH

○ Soft Finish   ○ Tart & Tingly   ○ Juicy & Fresh

LIFE IS TOO SHORT TO DRINK BAD WINE

WINE A BIT you'll feel better

R A T I N G

Appearance	☆ ☆ ☆ ☆ ☆
Aroma	☆ ☆ ☆ ☆ ☆
Body	☆ ☆ ☆ ☆ ☆
Taste	☆ ☆ ☆ ☆ ☆
Finish	☆ ☆ ☆ ☆ ☆
Overall Rating	☆ ☆ ☆ ☆ ☆

time to
wine down

Wine Name: _____
Winery: _____
Region: _____
Grapes: _____
Vintage: _____
Alcohol %: _____

KEEP CALM AND DRINK WINE

Wine Not?

⁘ Aroma ⁘

Primary Aromas: _____
Secondary Aromas: _____
Tertiary Aromas: _____

LOVE WINE

▬ Finish ▬

○ Soft Finish
○ Tart & Tingly
○ Juicy & Fresh

Tannin
LOW   MED   HIGH

Acidity
LOW   MED   HIGH

Body
LOW   MED   HIGH

★ Rating ★

Appearance	☆ ☆ ☆ ☆ ☆
Aroma	☆ ☆ ☆ ☆ ☆
Body	☆ ☆ ☆ ☆ ☆
Taste	☆ ☆ ☆ ☆ ☆
Finish	☆ ☆ ☆ ☆ ☆
Overall Rating	☆ ☆ ☆ ☆ ☆

Wine Name: _____

Winery: _____

Region: _____

Grapes: _____

Vintage: _____

Alcohol %: _____

Home is where ⊃THE WINE IS⊂

AROMA

Primary Aromas: _____

Secondary Aromas: _____

Tertiary Aromas: _____

TANNIN

LOW   MED   HIGH

ACIDITY

LOW   MED   HIGH

BODY

LOW   MED   HIGH

LIFE IS TOO SHORT TO DRINK BAD WINE

FINISH

◯ Soft Finish   ◯ Tart & Tingly   ◯ Juicy & Fresh

WINE A BIT *you'll feel better*

RATING

Appearance	☆ ☆ ☆ ☆ ☆
Aroma	☆ ☆ ☆ ☆ ☆
Body	☆ ☆ ☆ ☆ ☆
Taste	☆ ☆ ☆ ☆ ☆
Finish	☆ ☆ ☆ ☆ ☆
Overall Rating	☆ ☆ ☆ ☆ ☆

time to wine down

Wine Name: _____

Winery: _____

Region: _____

Grapes: _____

Vintage: _____

Alcohol %: _____

KEEP CALM AND DRINK WINE

Wine Not?

❧ Aroma ❧

Primary Aromas: _____

Secondary Aromas: _____

Tertiary Aromas: _____

LOVE WINE

▶ Finish ◀

- ○ Soft Finish
- ○ Tart & Tingly
- ○ Juicy & Fresh

Tannin

LOW   MED   HIGH

Acidity

LOW   MED   HIGH

Body

LOW   MED   HIGH

★ Rating ★

Appearance	☆ ☆ ☆ ☆ ☆
Aroma	☆ ☆ ☆ ☆ ☆
Body	☆ ☆ ☆ ☆ ☆
Taste	☆ ☆ ☆ ☆ ☆
Finish	☆ ☆ ☆ ☆ ☆
Overall Rating	☆ ☆ ☆ ☆ ☆

Home is where THE WINE IS

Wine Name: _____
Winery: _____
Region: _____
Grapes: _____
Vintage: _____
Alcohol %: _____

AROMA

Primary Aromas: _____
Secondary Aromas: _____
Tertiary Aromas: _____

TANNIN

LOW   MED   HIGH

ACIDITY

LOW   MED   HIGH

BODY

LOW   MED   HIGH

LIFE IS TOO SHORT TO DRINK BAD WINE

FINISH

○ Soft Finish   ○ Tart & Tingly   ○ Juicy & Fresh

WINE A BIT you'll feel better

RATING

Appearance	☆ ☆ ☆ ☆ ☆
Aroma	☆ ☆ ☆ ☆ ☆
Body	☆ ☆ ☆ ☆ ☆
Taste	☆ ☆ ☆ ☆ ☆
Finish	☆ ☆ ☆ ☆ ☆
Overall Rating	☆ ☆ ☆ ☆ ☆

time to wine down

Wine Name: _____

Winery: _____

Region: _____

Grapes: _____

Vintage: _____

Alcohol %: _____

KEEP CALM AND DRINK WINE

Wine Not?

❧ Aroma ❧

Primary Aromas: _____

Secondary Aromas: _____

Tertiary Aromas: _____

L♥VE WINE

Finish

O Soft Finish

O Tart & Tingly

O Juicy & Fresh

Tannin

LOW   MED   HIGH

Acidity

LOW   MED   HIGH

Body

LOW   MED   HIGH

★ Rating ★

Appearance	☆☆☆☆☆
Aroma	☆☆☆☆☆
Body	☆☆☆☆☆
Taste	☆☆☆☆☆
Finish	☆☆☆☆☆
Overall Rating	☆☆☆☆☆

Home is where THE WINE IS

Wine Name: _____

Winery: _____

Region: _____

Grapes: _____

Vintage: _____

Alcohol %: _____

AROMA

Primary Aromas: _____

Secondary Aromas: _____

Tertiary Aromas: _____

TANNIN
LOW   MED   HIGH

ACIDITY
LOW   MED   HIGH

BODY
LOW   MED   HIGH

LIFE IS TOO SHORT TO DRINK BAD WINE

FINISH

○ Soft Finish   ○ Tart & Tingly   ○ Juicy & Fresh

WINE A BIT you'll feel better

RATING

Appearance   ☆☆☆☆☆

Aroma   ☆☆☆☆☆

Body   ☆☆☆☆☆

Taste   ☆☆☆☆☆

Finish   ☆☆☆☆☆

Overall Rating ☆☆☆☆☆

time to
wine down

Wine Name: _____
Winery: _____
Region: _____
Grapes: _____
Vintage: _____
Alcohol %: _____

KEEP CALM AND DRINK WINE

Wine Not?

❈ Aroma ❈

Primary Aromas: _____
Secondary Aromas: _____
Tertiary Aromas: _____

L♥VE WINE

▶ Finish ◀

○ Soft Finish
○ Tart & Tingly
○ Juicy & Fresh

Tannin

LOW   MED   HIGH

Acidity

LOW   MED   HIGH

Body

LOW   MED   HIGH

★ Rating ★

Appearance	☆ ☆ ☆ ☆ ☆
Aroma	☆ ☆ ☆ ☆ ☆
Body	☆ ☆ ☆ ☆ ☆
Taste	☆ ☆ ☆ ☆ ☆
Finish	☆ ☆ ☆ ☆ ☆
Overall Rating	☆ ☆ ☆ ☆ ☆

Home is where THE WINE IS

Wine Name: _____

Winery: _____

Region: _____

Grapes: _____

Vintage: _____

Alcohol %: _____

AROMA

Primary Aromas: _____

Secondary Aromas: _____

Tertiary Aromas: _____

TANNIN

LOW   MED   HIGH

ACIDITY

LOW   MED   HIGH

BODY

LOW   MED   HIGH

LIFE IS TOO SHORT TO DRINK BAD WINE

FINISH

○ Soft Finish   ○ Tart & Tingly   ○ Juicy & Fresh

WINE A BIT you'll feel better

RATING

Appearance	☆ ☆ ☆ ☆ ☆
Aroma	☆ ☆ ☆ ☆ ☆
Body	☆ ☆ ☆ ☆ ☆
Taste	☆ ☆ ☆ ☆ ☆
Finish	☆ ☆ ☆ ☆ ☆
Overall Rating	☆ ☆ ☆ ☆ ☆

time to
wine down

Wine Name: _____

Winery: _____

Region: _____

Grapes: _____

Vintage: _____

Alcohol %: _____

KEEP CALM AND DRINK WINE

Wine Not?

Aroma

Primary Aromas: _____

Secondary Aromas: _____

Tertiary Aromas: _____

LOVE WINE

Finish
- ○ Soft Finish
- ○ Tart & Tingly
- ○ Juicy & Fresh

Tannin
LOW   MED   HIGH

Acidity
LOW   MED   HIGH

Body
LOW   MED   HIGH

★ Rating ★

Appearance	☆ ☆ ☆ ☆ ☆
Aroma	☆ ☆ ☆ ☆ ☆
Body	☆ ☆ ☆ ☆ ☆
Taste	☆ ☆ ☆ ☆ ☆
Finish	☆ ☆ ☆ ☆ ☆
Overall Rating	☆ ☆ ☆ ☆ ☆

Wine Name: _____

Winery: _____

Region: _____

Grapes: _____

Vintage: _____

Alcohol %: _____

AROMA

Primary Aromas: _____

Secondary Aromas: _____

Tertiary Aromas: _____

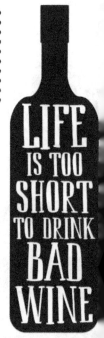

TANNIN

LOW   MED   HIGH

ACIDITY

LOW   MED   HIGH

BODY

LOW   MED   HIGH

FINISH

○ Soft Finish   ○ Tart & Tingly   ○ Juicy & Fresh

WINE A BIT
you'll feel better

RATING

Appearance	☆☆☆☆☆
Aroma	☆☆☆☆☆
Body	☆☆☆☆☆
Taste	☆☆☆☆☆
Finish	☆☆☆☆☆
Overall Rating	☆☆☆☆☆

time to
wine down

Wine Name: _____

Winery: _____

Region: _____

Grapes: _____

Vintage: _____

Alcohol %: _____

KEEP CALM AND DRINK WINE

Aroma

Wine Not?

Primary Aromas: _____

Secondary Aromas: _____

Tertiary Aromas: _____

LOVE WINE

Finish

○ Soft Finish

○ Tart & Tingly

○ Juicy & Fresh

Tannin

LOW	MED	HIGH

Acidity

LOW	MED	HIGH

Body

LOW	MED	HIGH

★ Rating ★

Appearance	☆ ☆ ☆ ☆ ☆
Aroma	☆ ☆ ☆ ☆ ☆
Body	☆ ☆ ☆ ☆ ☆
Taste	☆ ☆ ☆ ☆ ☆
Finish	☆ ☆ ☆ ☆ ☆
Overall Rating	☆ ☆ ☆ ☆ ☆

Wine Name: _____

Winery: _____

Region: _____

Grapes: _____

Vintage: _____

Alcohol %: _____

AROMA

Primary Aromas: _____

Secondary Aromas: _____

Tertiary Aromas: _____

TANNIN

LOW   MED   HIGH

ACIDITY

LOW   MED   HIGH

BODY

LOW   MED   HIGH

FINISH

○ Soft Finish   ○ Tart & Tingly   ○ Juicy & Fresh

LIFE IS TOO SHORT TO DRINK BAD WINE

WINE A BIT *you'll feel better*

RATING		
Appearance	☆☆☆☆☆
Aroma	☆☆☆☆☆
Body	☆☆☆☆☆
Taste	☆☆☆☆☆
Finish	☆☆☆☆☆
Overall Rating	☆☆☆☆☆

time to
wine down

Wine Name: _____

Winery: _____

Region: _____

Grapes: _____

Vintage: _____

Alcohol %: _____

KEEP CALM AND DRINK WINE

Wine Not?

Aroma

Primary Aromas: _____

Secondary Aromas: _____

Tertiary Aromas: _____

LOVE WINE

Finish

○ Soft Finish

○ Tart & Tingly

○ Juicy & Fresh

Tannin

LOW — MED — HIGH

Acidity

LOW — MED — HIGH

Body

LOW — MED — HIGH

★ Rating ★

Appearance	☆ ☆ ☆ ☆ ☆
Aroma	☆ ☆ ☆ ☆ ☆
Body	☆ ☆ ☆ ☆ ☆
Taste	☆ ☆ ☆ ☆ ☆
Finish	☆ ☆ ☆ ☆ ☆
Overall Rating	☆ ☆ ☆ ☆ ☆

Home is where THE WINE IS

Wine Name: _____

Winery: _____

Region: _____

Grapes: _____

Vintage: _____

Alcohol %: _____

AROMA

Primary Aromas: _____

Secondary Aromas: _____

Tertiary Aromas: _____

TANNIN
LOW   MED   HIGH

ACIDITY
LOW   MED   HIGH

BODY
LOW   MED   HIGH

LIFE IS TOO SHORT TO DRINK BAD WINE

FINISH

○ Soft Finish   ○ Tart & Tingly   ○ Juicy & Fresh

WINE A BIT you'll feel better

RATING

Appearance	☆ ☆ ☆ ☆ ☆
Aroma	☆ ☆ ☆ ☆ ☆
Body	☆ ☆ ☆ ☆ ☆
Taste	☆ ☆ ☆ ☆ ☆
Finish	☆ ☆ ☆ ☆ ☆
Overall Rating	☆ ☆ ☆ ☆ ☆

time to wine down

Wine Name: _____

Winery: _____

Region: _____

Grapes: _____

Vintage: _____

Alcohol %: _____

KEEP CALM AND DRINK WINE

Wine Not?

Aroma

Primary Aromas: _____

Secondary Aromas: _____

Tertiary Aromas: _____

LOVE WINE

Finish

- ○ Soft Finish
- ○ Tart & Tingly
- ○ Juicy & Fresh

Tannin

LOW   MED   HIGH

Acidity

LOW   MED   HIGH

Body

LOW   MED   HIGH

★ Rating ★

Appearance	☆ ☆ ☆ ☆ ☆
Aroma	☆ ☆ ☆ ☆ ☆
Body	☆ ☆ ☆ ☆ ☆
Taste	☆ ☆ ☆ ☆ ☆
Finish	☆ ☆ ☆ ☆ ☆
Overall Rating	☆ ☆ ☆ ☆ ☆

Wine Name: _____

Winery: _____

Region: _____

Grapes: _____

Vintage: _____

Alcohol %: _____

AROMA

Primary Aromas: _____

Secondary Aromas: _____

Tertiary Aromas: _____

TANNIN

LOW   MED   HIGH

ACIDITY

LOW   MED   HIGH

BODY

LOW   MED   HIGH

LIFE IS TOO SHORT TO DRINK BAD WINE

FINISH

○ Soft Finish   ○ Tart & Tingly   ○ Juicy & Fresh

WINE A BIT you'll feel better

RATING

Appearance	☆☆☆☆☆
Aroma	☆☆☆☆☆
Body	☆☆☆☆☆
Taste	☆☆☆☆☆
Finish	☆☆☆☆☆
Overall Rating	☆☆☆☆☆

Home is where THE WINE IS

time to **wine down**

Wine Name: _____

Winery: _____

Region: _____

Grapes: _____

Vintage: _____

Alcohol %: _____

KEEP CALM AND DRINK WINE

Aroma

Primary Aromas: _____

Secondary Aromas: _____

Tertiary Aromas: _____

Wine Not?

L♥VE WINE

Finish

O Soft Finish

O Tart & Tingly

O Juicy & Fresh

Tannin

LOW — MED — HIGH

Acidity

LOW — MED — HIGH

Body

LOW — MED — HIGH

★ Rating ★

Appearance	☆☆☆☆☆
Aroma	☆☆☆☆☆
Body	☆☆☆☆☆
Taste	☆☆☆☆☆
Finish	☆☆☆☆☆
Overall Rating	☆☆☆☆☆

Wine Name: _____

Winery: _____

Region: _____

Grapes: _____

Vintage: _____

Alcohol %: _____

Home is where =THE WINE IS=

AROMA

Primary Aromas: _____

Secondary Aromas: _____

Tertiary Aromas: _____

TANNIN

LOW   MED   HIGH

ACIDITY

LOW   MED   HIGH

BODY

LOW   MED   HIGH

FINISH

○ Soft Finish   ○ Tart & Tingly   ○ Juicy & Fresh

LIFE IS TOO SHORT TO DRINK BAD WINE

WINE A BIT
you'll feel better

RATING

Appearance	☆ ☆ ☆ ☆ ☆
Aroma	☆ ☆ ☆ ☆ ☆
Body	☆ ☆ ☆ ☆ ☆
Taste	☆ ☆ ☆ ☆ ☆
Finish	☆ ☆ ☆ ☆ ☆
Overall Rating	☆ ☆ ☆ ☆ ☆

time to wine down

Wine Name: _____

Winery: _____

Region: _____

Grapes: _____

Vintage: _____

Alcohol %: _____

KEEP CALM AND DRINK WINE

Wine Not?

Aroma

Primary Aromas: _____

Secondary Aromas: _____

Tertiary Aromas: _____

LOVE WINE

Finish

○ Soft Finish
○ Tart & Tingly
○ Juicy & Fresh

Tannin

LOW   MED   HIGH

Acidity

LOW   MED   HIGH

Body

LOW   MED   HIGH

★ Rating ★

Appearance	☆ ☆ ☆ ☆ ☆
Aroma	☆ ☆ ☆ ☆ ☆
Body	☆ ☆ ☆ ☆ ☆
Taste	☆ ☆ ☆ ☆ ☆
Finish	☆ ☆ ☆ ☆ ☆
Overall Rating	☆ ☆ ☆ ☆ ☆

Home is where
THE WINE IS

Wine Name: _____
Winery: _____
Region: _____
Grapes: _____
Vintage: _____
Alcohol %: _____

AROMA

Primary Aromas: _____
Secondary Aromas: _____
Tertiary Aromas: _____

TANNIN
LOW   MED   HIGH

ACIDITY
LOW   MED   HIGH

BODY
LOW   MED   HIGH

FINISH

○ Soft Finish   ○ Tart & Tingly   ○ Juicy & Fresh

LIFE IS TOO SHORT TO DRINK BAD WINE

WINE A BIT
you'll feel better

RATING

Appearance	☆☆☆☆☆
Aroma	☆☆☆☆☆
Body	☆☆☆☆☆
Taste	☆☆☆☆☆
Finish	☆☆☆☆☆
Overall Rating	☆☆☆☆☆

time to
wine down

Wine Name: _____

Winery: _____

Region: _____

Grapes: _____

Vintage: _____

Alcohol %: _____

KEEP CALM AND DRINK WINE

Wine Not?

Aroma

Primary Aromas: _____

Secondary Aromas: _____

Tertiary Aromas: _____

LOVE WINE

Finish
- ○ Soft Finish
- ○ Tart & Tingly
- ○ Juicy & Fresh

Tannin

OW   MED   HIGH

Acidity

OW   MED   HIGH

Body

OW   MED   HIGH

★ Rating ★

Appearance	☆ ☆ ☆ ☆ ☆
Aroma	☆ ☆ ☆ ☆ ☆
Body	☆ ☆ ☆ ☆ ☆
Taste	☆ ☆ ☆ ☆ ☆
Finish	☆ ☆ ☆ ☆ ☆
Overall Rating	☆ ☆ ☆ ☆ ☆

Home is where THE WINE IS

Wine Name: _____

Winery: _____

Region: _____

Grapes: _____

Vintage: _____

Alcohol %: _____

AROMA

Primary Aromas: _____

Secondary Aromas: _____

Tertiary Aromas: _____

LIFE IS TOO SHORT TO DRINK BAD WINE

TANNIN
LOW   MED   HIGH

ACIDITY
LOW   MED   HIGH

BODY
LOW   MED   HIGH

FINISH

○ Soft Finish   ○ Tart & Tingly   ○ Juicy & Fresh

WINE A BIT you'll feel better

RATING

Appearance	☆ ☆ ☆ ☆ ☆
Aroma	☆ ☆ ☆ ☆ ☆
Body	☆ ☆ ☆ ☆ ☆
Taste	☆ ☆ ☆ ☆ ☆
Finish	☆ ☆ ☆ ☆ ☆
Overall Rating	☆ ☆ ☆ ☆ ☆

time to
wine down

Wine Name: _____

Winery: _____

Region: _____

Grapes: _____

Vintage: _____

Alcohol %: _____

KEEP CALM AND DRINK WINE

Wine Not?

☙ Aroma ❧

Primary Aromas: _____

Secondary Aromas: _____

Tertiary Aromas: _____

L♥VE WINE

Finish

- ○ Soft Finish
- ○ Tart & Tingly
- ○ Juicy & Fresh

Tannin

LOW   MED   HIGH

Acidity

LOW   MED   HIGH

Body

LOW   MED   HIGH

★ Rating ★

Appearance	☆ ☆ ☆ ☆ ☆
Aroma	☆ ☆ ☆ ☆ ☆
Body	☆ ☆ ☆ ☆ ☆
Taste	☆ ☆ ☆ ☆ ☆
Finish	☆ ☆ ☆ ☆ ☆
Overall Rating	☆ ☆ ☆ ☆ ☆

Home is where THE WINE IS

Wine Name: _____
Winery: _____
Region: _____
Grapes: _____
Vintage: _____
Alcohol %: _____

AROMA

Primary Aromas: _____
Secondary Aromas: _____
Tertiary Aromas: _____

TANNIN

LOW   MED   HIGH

ACIDITY

LOW   MED   HIGH

BODY

LOW   MED   HIGH

FINISH

○ Soft Finish   ○ Tart & Tingly   ○ Juicy & Fresh

LIFE IS TOO SHORT TO DRINK BAD WINE

WINE A BIT
you'll feel better

RATING

Appearance	☆ ☆ ☆ ☆ ☆
Aroma	☆ ☆ ☆ ☆ ☆
Body	☆ ☆ ☆ ☆ ☆
Taste	☆ ☆ ☆ ☆ ☆
Finish	☆ ☆ ☆ ☆ ☆
Overall Rating	☆ ☆ ☆ ☆ ☆

time to wine down

Wine Name: _____

Winery: _____

Region: _____

Grapes: _____

Vintage: _____

Alcohol %: _____

KEEP CALM AND DRINK WINE

Wine Not?

Aroma

Primary Aromas: _____

Secondary Aromas: _____

Tertiary Aromas: _____

LOVE WINE

Finish

○ Soft Finish

○ Tart & Tingly

○ Juicy & Fresh

Tannin

LOW   MED   HIGH

Acidity

LOW   MED   HIGH

Body

LOW   MED   HIGH

★ Rating ★

Appearance	☆ ☆ ☆ ☆ ☆
Aroma	☆ ☆ ☆ ☆ ☆
Body	☆ ☆ ☆ ☆ ☆
Taste	☆ ☆ ☆ ☆ ☆
Finish	☆ ☆ ☆ ☆ ☆
Overall Rating	☆ ☆ ☆ ☆ ☆

Wine Name: _____

Winery: _____

Region: _____

Grapes: _____

Vintage: _____

Alcohol %: _____

AROMA

Primary Aromas: _____

Secondary Aromas: _____

Tertiary Aromas: _____

TANNIN
LOW   MED   HIGH

ACIDITY
LOW   MED   HIGH

BODY
LOW   MED   HIGH

FINISH

○ Soft Finish   ○ Tart & Tingly   ○ Juicy & Fresh

LIFE IS TOO SHORT TO DRINK BAD WINE

WINE A BIT you'll feel better

RATING

Appearance	☆☆☆☆☆
Aroma	☆☆☆☆☆
Body	☆☆☆☆☆
Taste	☆☆☆☆☆
Finish	☆☆☆☆☆
Overall Rating	☆☆☆☆☆

Home is where THE WINE IS

time to wine down

Wine Name: _____

Winery: _____

Region: _____

Grapes: _____

Vintage: _____

Alcohol %: _____

KEEP CALM AND DRINK WINE

Wine Not?

Aroma

Primary Aromas: _____

Secondary Aromas: _____

Tertiary Aromas: _____

LOVE WINE

Finish

O Soft Finish

O Tart & Tingly

O Juicy & Fresh

Tannin

LOW   MED   HIGH

Acidity

LOW   MED   HIGH

Body

LOW   MED   HIGH

★ Rating ★

Appearance	☆ ☆ ☆ ☆ ☆
Aroma	☆ ☆ ☆ ☆ ☆
Body	☆ ☆ ☆ ☆ ☆
Taste	☆ ☆ ☆ ☆ ☆
Finish	☆ ☆ ☆ ☆ ☆
Overall Rating	☆ ☆ ☆ ☆ ☆

Wine Name: _____

Winery: _____

Region: _____

Grapes: _____

Vintage: _____

Alcohol %: _____

Home is where
=THE WINE IS=

AROMA

Primary Aromas: _____

Secondary Aromas: _____

Tertiary Aromas: _____

TANNIN

LOW   MED   HIGH

ACIDITY

LOW   MED   HIGH

BODY

LOW   MED   HIGH

FINISH

○ Soft Finish   ○ Tart & Tingly   ○ Juicy & Fresh

LIFE IS TOO SHORT TO DRINK BAD WINE

WINE A BIT
you'll feel better

RATING

Appearance	☆ ☆ ☆ ☆ ☆
Aroma	☆ ☆ ☆ ☆ ☆
Body	☆ ☆ ☆ ☆ ☆
Taste	☆ ☆ ☆ ☆ ☆
Finish	☆ ☆ ☆ ☆ ☆
Overall Rating	☆ ☆ ☆ ☆ ☆

time to
wine down

Wine Name: _____

Winery: _____

Region: _____

Grapes: _____

Vintage: _____

Alcohol %: _____

KEEP CALM AND DRINK WINE

Wine Not?

❦ Aroma ❦

Primary Aromas: _____

Secondary Aromas: _____

Tertiary Aromas: _____

L♥VE WINE

▬ Finish ▬

○ Soft Finish

○ Tart & Tingly

○ Juicy & Fresh

Tannin

LOW   MED   HIGH

Acidity

LOW   MED   HIGH

Body

LOW   MED   HIGH

★ Rating ★

Appearance	☆☆☆☆☆
Aroma	☆☆☆☆☆
Body	☆☆☆☆☆
Taste	☆☆☆☆☆
Finish	☆☆☆☆☆
Overall Rating	☆☆☆☆☆

Wine Name: _____

Winery: _____

Region: _____

Grapes: _____

Vintage: _____

Alcohol %: _____

AROMA

Primary Aromas: _____

Secondary Aromas: _____

Tertiary Aromas: _____

TANNIN

LOW   MED   HIGH

ACIDITY

LOW   MED   HIGH

BODY

LOW   MED   HIGH

FINISH

○ Soft Finish   ○ Tart & Tingly   ○ Juicy & Fresh

RATING

Appearance	☆☆☆☆☆
Aroma	☆☆☆☆☆
Body	☆☆☆☆☆
Taste	☆☆☆☆☆
Finish	☆☆☆☆☆
Overall Rating	☆☆☆☆☆

time to wine down

Wine Name: _____

Winery: _____

Region: _____

Grapes: _____

Vintage: _____

Alcohol %: _____

KEEP CALM AND DRINK WINE

Aroma

Primary Aromas: _____

Secondary Aromas: _____

Tertiary Aromas: _____

Wine Not?

LOVE WINE

Finish

- ○ Soft Finish
- ○ Tart & Tingly
- ○ Juicy & Fresh

Tannin

LOW   MED   HIGH

Acidity

LOW   MED   HIGH

Body

LOW   MED   HIGH

★ Rating ★

Appearance	☆ ☆ ☆ ☆ ☆
Aroma	☆ ☆ ☆ ☆ ☆
Body	☆ ☆ ☆ ☆ ☆
Taste	☆ ☆ ☆ ☆ ☆
Finish	☆ ☆ ☆ ☆ ☆
Overall Rating	☆ ☆ ☆ ☆ ☆

Home is where THE WINE IS

Wine Name: _____

Winery: _____

Region: _____

Grapes: _____

Vintage: _____

Alcohol %: _____

AROMA

Primary Aromas: _____

Secondary Aromas: _____

Tertiary Aromas: _____

TANNIN
LOW   MED   HIGH

ACIDITY
LOW   MED   HIGH

BODY
LOW   MED   HIGH

LIFE IS TOO SHORT TO DRINK BAD WINE

FINISH

○ Soft Finish   ○ Tart & Tingly   ○ Juicy & Fresh

WINE A BIT you'll feel better

RATING

Appearance	☆ ☆ ☆ ☆ ☆
Aroma	☆ ☆ ☆ ☆ ☆
Body	☆ ☆ ☆ ☆ ☆
Taste	☆ ☆ ☆ ☆ ☆
Finish	☆ ☆ ☆ ☆ ☆
Overall Rating	☆ ☆ ☆ ☆ ☆

time to wine down

Wine Name: _____

Winery: _____

Region: _____

Grapes: _____

Vintage: _____

Alcohol %: _____

KEEP CALM AND DRINK WINE

Wine Not?

Aroma

Primary Aromas: _____

Secondary Aromas: _____

Tertiary Aromas: _____

LOVE WINE

Finish

O Soft Finish

O Tart & Tingly

O Juicy & Fresh

Tannin

LOW   MED   HIGH

Acidity

LOW   MED   HIGH

Body

LOW   MED   HIGH

★ Rating ★

Appearance	☆ ☆ ☆ ☆ ☆
Aroma	☆ ☆ ☆ ☆ ☆
Body	☆ ☆ ☆ ☆ ☆
Taste	☆ ☆ ☆ ☆ ☆
Finish	☆ ☆ ☆ ☆ ☆
Overall Rating	☆ ☆ ☆ ☆ ☆

Home is where THE WINE IS

Wine Name: _____

Winery: _____

Region: _____

Grapes: _____

Vintage: _____

Alcohol %: _____

AROMA

Primary Aromas: _____

Secondary Aromas: _____

Tertiary Aromas: _____

TANNIN
LOW   MED   HIGH

ACIDITY
LOW   MED   HIGH

BODY
LOW   MED   HIGH

FINISH

○ Soft Finish   ○ Tart & Tingly   ○ Juicy & Fresh

LIFE IS TOO SHORT TO DRINK BAD WINE

WINE A BIT you'll feel better

RATING

Appearance	☆ ☆ ☆ ☆ ☆
Aroma	☆ ☆ ☆ ☆ ☆
Body	☆ ☆ ☆ ☆ ☆
Taste	☆ ☆ ☆ ☆ ☆
Finish	☆ ☆ ☆ ☆ ☆
Overall Rating	☆ ☆ ☆ ☆ ☆

time to wine down

Wine Name: _____

Winery: _____

Region: _____

Grapes: _____

Vintage: _____

Alcohol %: _____

KEEP CALM AND DRINK WINE

Wine Not?

❧ Aroma ❧

Primary Aromas: _____

Secondary Aromas: _____

Tertiary Aromas: _____

LOVE WINE

Finish

○ Soft Finish

○ Tart & Tingly

○ Juicy & Fresh

Tannin

LOW   MED   HIGH

Acidity

LOW   MED   HIGH

Body

LOW   MED   HIGH

★ Rating ★

Appearance	☆ ☆ ☆ ☆ ☆
Aroma	☆ ☆ ☆ ☆ ☆
Body	☆ ☆ ☆ ☆ ☆
Taste	☆ ☆ ☆ ☆ ☆
Finish	☆ ☆ ☆ ☆ ☆
Overall Rating	☆ ☆ ☆ ☆ ☆

Home is where
≥THE WINE IS≤

Wine Name: _____
Winery: _____
Region: _____
Grapes: _____
Vintage: _____
Alcohol %: _____

AROMA

Primary Aromas: _____
Secondary Aromas: _____
Tertiary Aromas: _____

LIFE IS TOO SHORT TO DRINK BAD WINE

TANNIN
LOW   MED   HIGH

ACIDITY
LOW   MED   HIGH

BODY
LOW   MED   HIGH

FINISH

○ Soft Finish   ○ Tart & Tingly   ○ Juicy & Fresh

WINE A BIT
you'll feel better

RATING

Appearance	☆ ☆ ☆ ☆ ☆
Aroma	☆ ☆ ☆ ☆ ☆
Body	☆ ☆ ☆ ☆ ☆
Taste	☆ ☆ ☆ ☆ ☆
Finish	☆ ☆ ☆ ☆ ☆
Overall Rating	☆ ☆ ☆ ☆ ☆

time to wine down

Wine Name: _____

Winery: _____

Region: _____

Grapes: _____

Vintage: _____

Alcohol %: _____

KEEP CALM AND DRINK WINE

Wine Not?

Aroma

Primary Aromas: _____

Secondary Aromas: _____

Tertiary Aromas: _____

LOVE WINE

Finish

○ Soft Finish

○ Tart & Tingly

○ Juicy & Fresh

Tannin

LOW   MED   HIGH

Acidity

LOW   MED   HIGH

Body

LOW   MED   HIGH

★ Rating ★

Appearance	☆ ☆ ☆ ☆ ☆
Aroma	☆ ☆ ☆ ☆ ☆
Body	☆ ☆ ☆ ☆ ☆
Taste	☆ ☆ ☆ ☆ ☆
Finish	☆ ☆ ☆ ☆ ☆
Overall Rating	☆ ☆ ☆ ☆ ☆

Home is where =THE WINE IS=

Wine Name: _____

Winery: _____

Region: _____

Grapes: _____

Vintage: _____

Alcohol %: _____

AROMA

Primary Aromas: _____

Secondary Aromas: _____

Tertiary Aromas: _____

TANNIN

LOW   MED   HIGH

ACIDITY

LOW   MED   HIGH

BODY

LOW   MED   HIGH

FINISH

○ Soft Finish   ○ Tart & Tingly   ○ Juicy & Fresh

LIFE IS TOO SHORT TO DRINK BAD WINE

WINE A BIT you'll feel better

RATING		
Appearance	☆☆☆☆☆
Aroma	☆☆☆☆☆
Body	☆☆☆☆☆
Taste	☆☆☆☆☆
Finish	☆☆☆☆☆
Overall Rating	☆☆☆☆☆

time to
wine down

Wine Name: _____

Winery: _____

Region: _____

Grapes: _____

Vintage: _____

Alcohol %: _____

KEEP CALM AND DRINK WINE

✿ Aroma ✿

Wine Not?

Primary Aromas: _____

Secondary Aromas: _____

Tertiary Aromas: _____

LOVE WINE

➤ Finish ◄

○ Soft Finish

○ Tart & Tingly

○ Juicy & Fresh

Tannin

LOW — MED — HIGH

Acidity

LOW — MED — HIGH

Body

LOW — MED — HIGH

★ Rating ★

Appearance	☆ ☆ ☆ ☆ ☆
Aroma	☆ ☆ ☆ ☆ ☆
Body	☆ ☆ ☆ ☆ ☆
Taste	☆ ☆ ☆ ☆ ☆
Finish	☆ ☆ ☆ ☆ ☆
Overall Rating	☆ ☆ ☆ ☆ ☆

Home is where
THE WINE IS

Wine Name: _____
Winery: _____
Region: _____
Grapes: _____
Vintage: _____
Alcohol %: _____

AROMA

Primary Aromas: _____
Secondary Aromas: _____
Tertiary Aromas: _____

TANNIN
LOW   MED   HIGH

ACIDITY
LOW   MED   HIGH

BODY
LOW   MED   HIGH

FINISH

◯ Soft Finish   ◯ Tart & Tingly   ◯ Juicy & Fresh

LIFE IS TOO SHORT TO DRINK BAD WINE

WINE A BIT
you'll feel better

RATING		
Appearance	☆☆☆☆☆
Aroma	☆☆☆☆☆
Body	☆☆☆☆☆
Taste	☆☆☆☆☆
Finish	☆☆☆☆☆
Overall Rating	☆☆☆☆☆

time to
wine down

Wine Name: _____

Winery: _____

Region: _____

Grapes: _____

Vintage: _____

Alcohol %: _____

KEEP CALM AND DRINK WINE

Wine Not?

Aroma

Primary Aromas: _____

Secondary Aromas: _____

Tertiary Aromas: _____

LOVE WINE

Finish

○ Soft Finish

○ Tart & Tingly

○ Juicy & Fresh

Tannin

LOW   MED   HIGH

Acidity

LOW   MED   HIGH

Body

LOW   MED   HIGH

★ Rating ★

Appearance	☆ ☆ ☆ ☆ ☆
Aroma	☆ ☆ ☆ ☆ ☆
Body	☆ ☆ ☆ ☆ ☆
Taste	☆ ☆ ☆ ☆ ☆
Finish	☆ ☆ ☆ ☆ ☆
Overall Rating	☆ ☆ ☆ ☆ ☆

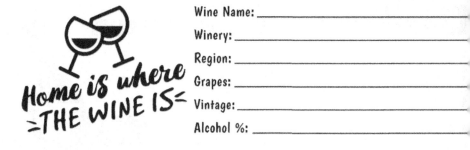

Wine Name: _____

Winery: _____

Region: _____

Grapes: _____

Vintage: _____

Alcohol %: _____

AROMA

Primary Aromas: _____

Secondary Aromas: _____

Tertiary Aromas: _____

TANNIN
LOW   MED   HIGH

ACIDITY
LOW   MED   HIGH

BODY
LOW   MED   HIGH

FINISH

○ Soft Finish   ○ Tart & Tingly   ○ Juicy & Fresh

WINE A BIT
you'll feel better

RATING

Appearance	☆☆☆☆☆
Aroma	☆☆☆☆☆
Body	☆☆☆☆☆
Taste	☆☆☆☆☆
Finish	☆☆☆☆☆
Overall Rating	☆☆☆☆☆

time to
wine down

Wine Name: ______________________________

Winery: ______________________________

Region: ______________________________

Grapes: ______________________________

Vintage: ______________________________

Alcohol %: ______________________________

KEEP CALM AND DRINK WINE

Wine Not?

Aroma

Primary Aromas: ______________________________

Secondary Aromas: ______________________________

Tertiary Aromas: ______________________________

LOVE WINE

Finish

- ☐ Soft Finish
- ☐ Tart & Tingly
- ☐ Juicy & Fresh

Tannin

LOW ——— MED ——— HIGH

Acidity

LOW ——— MED ——— HIGH

Body

LOW ——— MED ——— HIGH

★ Rating ★

Appearance	☆☆☆☆☆
Aroma	☆☆☆☆☆
Body	☆☆☆☆☆
Taste	☆☆☆☆☆
Finish	☆☆☆☆☆
Overall Rating	☆☆☆☆☆

Wine Name: _____

Winery: _____

Region: _____

Grapes: _____

Vintage: _____

Alcohol %: _____

Home is where
≥THE WINE IS≤

AROMA

Primary Aromas: _____

Secondary Aromas: _____

Tertiary Aromas: _____

LIFE IS TOO SHORT TO DRINK BAD WINE

TANNIN
LOW   MED   HIGH

ACIDITY
LOW   MED   HIGH

BODY
LOW   MED   HIGH

FINISH

○ Soft Finish   ○ Tart & Tingly   ○ Juicy & Fresh

WINE A BIT
you'll feel better

RATING

Appearance	☆ ☆ ☆ ☆ ☆
Aroma	☆ ☆ ☆ ☆ ☆
Body	☆ ☆ ☆ ☆ ☆
Taste	☆ ☆ ☆ ☆ ☆
Finish	☆ ☆ ☆ ☆ ☆
Overall Rating	☆ ☆ ☆ ☆ ☆

time to
wine down

Wine Name: _____

Winery: _____

Region: _____

Grapes: _____

Vintage: _____

Alcohol %: _____

KEEP CALM AND DRINK WINE

Wine Not?

Aroma

Primary Aromas: _____

Secondary Aromas: _____

Tertiary Aromas: _____

LOVE WINE

Finish

○ Soft Finish
○ Tart & Tingly
○ Juicy & Fresh

Tannin

LOW   MED   HIGH

Acidity

LOW   MED   HIGH

Body

LOW   MED   HIGH

★ Rating ★

Appearance	☆ ☆ ☆ ☆ ☆
Aroma	☆ ☆ ☆ ☆ ☆
Body	☆ ☆ ☆ ☆ ☆
Taste	☆ ☆ ☆ ☆ ☆
Finish	☆ ☆ ☆ ☆ ☆
Overall Rating	☆ ☆ ☆ ☆ ☆

Wine Name: _____

Winery: _____

Region: _____

Grapes: _____

Vintage: _____

Alcohol %: _____

Home is where THE WINE IS

AROMA

Primary Aromas: _____

Secondary Aromas: _____

Tertiary Aromas: _____

 TANNIN

LOW   MED   HIGH

 ACIDITY

LOW   MED   HIGH

 BODY

LOW   MED   HIGH

FINISH

○ Soft Finish   ○ Tart & Tingly   ○ Juicy & Fresh

LIFE IS TOO SHORT TO DRINK BAD WINE

WINE A BIT *you'll feel better*

RATING

Appearance	☆☆☆☆☆
Aroma	☆☆☆☆☆
Body	☆☆☆☆☆
Taste	☆☆☆☆☆
Finish	☆☆☆☆☆
Overall Rating	☆☆☆☆☆

time to
wine down

Wine Name: _____

Winery: _____

Region: _____

Grapes: _____

Vintage: _____

Alcohol %: _____

KEEP CALM AND DRINK WINE

Wine Not?

Aroma

Primary Aromas: _____

Secondary Aromas: _____

Tertiary Aromas: _____

LOVE WINE

Finish

○ Soft Finish

○ Tart & Tingly

○ Juicy & Fresh

Tannin

LOW   MED   HIGH

Acidity

LOW   MED   HIGH

Body

LOW   MED   HIGH

Rating

Appearance	☆ ☆ ☆ ☆ ☆
Aroma	☆ ☆ ☆ ☆ ☆
Body	☆ ☆ ☆ ☆ ☆
Taste	☆ ☆ ☆ ☆ ☆
Finish	☆ ☆ ☆ ☆ ☆
Overall Rating	☆ ☆ ☆ ☆ ☆

Wine Name: _____

Winery: _____

Region: _____

Grapes: _____

Vintage: _____

Alcohol %: _____

AROMA

Primary Aromas: _____

Secondary Aromas: _____

Tertiary Aromas: _____

TANNIN
LOW   MED   HIGH

ACIDITY
LOW   MED   HIGH

BODY
LOW   MED   HIGH

LIFE IS TOO SHORT TO DRINK BAD WINE

FINISH

○ Soft Finish   ○ Tart & Tingly   ○ Juicy & Fresh

RATING

Appearance	☆ ☆ ☆ ☆ ☆
Aroma	☆ ☆ ☆ ☆ ☆
Body	☆ ☆ ☆ ☆ ☆
Taste	☆ ☆ ☆ ☆ ☆
Finish	☆ ☆ ☆ ☆ ☆
Overall Rating	☆ ☆ ☆ ☆ ☆

time to wine down

Wine Name: _____

Winery: _____

Region: _____

Grapes: _____

Vintage: _____

Alcohol %: _____

KEEP CALM AND DRINK WINE

Wine Not?

Aroma

Primary Aromas: _____

Secondary Aromas: _____

Tertiary Aromas: _____

LOVE WINE

Finish

○ Soft Finish
○ Tart & Tingly
○ Juicy & Fresh

Tannin

LOW   MED   HIGH

Acidity

LOW   MED   HIGH

Body

LOW   MED   HIGH

Rating

Appearance	☆ ☆ ☆ ☆ ☆
Aroma	☆ ☆ ☆ ☆ ☆
Body	☆ ☆ ☆ ☆ ☆
Taste	☆ ☆ ☆ ☆ ☆
Finish	☆ ☆ ☆ ☆ ☆
Overall Rating	☆ ☆ ☆ ☆ ☆

Wine Name: _____

Winery: _____

Region: _____

Grapes: _____

Vintage: _____

Alcohol %: _____

AROMA

Primary Aromas: _____

Secondary Aromas: _____

Tertiary Aromas: _____

TANNIN
LOW   MED   HIGH

ACIDITY
LOW   MED   HIGH

BODY
LOW   MED   HIGH

FINISH

○ Soft Finish   ○ Tart & Tingly   ○ Juicy & Fresh

RATING

Appearance	☆ ☆ ☆ ☆ ☆
Aroma	☆ ☆ ☆ ☆ ☆
Body	☆ ☆ ☆ ☆ ☆
Taste	☆ ☆ ☆ ☆ ☆
Finish	☆ ☆ ☆ ☆ ☆
Overall Rating	☆ ☆ ☆ ☆ ☆

time to
wine down

Wine Name: _____

Winery: _____

Region: _____

Grapes: _____

Vintage: _____

Alcohol %: _____

KEEP CALM AND DRINK WINE

Wine Not?

Aroma

Primary Aromas: _____

Secondary Aromas: _____

Tertiary Aromas: _____

LOVE WINE

Finish

- ○ Soft Finish
- ○ Tart & Tingly
- ○ Juicy & Fresh

Tannin

LOW   MED   HIGH

Acidity

LOW   MED   HIGH

Body

LOW   MED   HIGH

★ Rating ★

Appearance	☆	☆	☆	☆	☆
Aroma	☆	☆	☆	☆	☆
Body	☆	☆	☆	☆	☆
Taste	☆	☆	☆	☆	☆
Finish	☆	☆	☆	☆	☆
Overall Rating	☆	☆	☆	☆	☆

Wine Name: _____

Winery: _____

Region: _____

Grapes: _____

Vintage: _____

Alcohol %: _____

Home is where
>THE WINE IS<

AROMA

Primary Aromas: _____

Secondary Aromas: _____

Tertiary Aromas: _____

TANNIN
LOW   MED   HIGH

ACIDITY
LOW   MED   HIGH

BODY
LOW   MED   HIGH

LIFE IS TOO SHORT TO DRINK BAD WINE

FINISH

○ Soft Finish   ○ Tart & Tingly   ○ Juicy & Fresh

WINE A BIT
you'll feel better

RATING

Appearance	☆☆☆☆☆
Aroma	☆☆☆☆☆
Body	☆☆☆☆☆
Taste	☆☆☆☆☆
Finish	☆☆☆☆☆
Overall Rating	☆☆☆☆☆

time to wine down

Wine Name: _____

Winery: _____

Region: _____

Grapes: _____

Vintage: _____

Alcohol %: _____

KEEP CALM AND DRINK WINE

Wine Not?

❋ Aroma ❋

Primary Aromas: _____

Secondary Aromas: _____

Tertiary Aromas: _____

L♥VE W♥NE

Finish

O Soft Finish

O Tart & Tingly

O Juicy & Fresh

Tannin

LOW   MED   HIGH

Acidity

LOW   MED   HIGH

Body

LOW   MED   HIGH

★ Rating ★

Appearance	☆ ☆ ☆ ☆ ☆
Aroma	☆ ☆ ☆ ☆ ☆
Body	☆ ☆ ☆ ☆ ☆
Taste	☆ ☆ ☆ ☆ ☆
Finish	☆ ☆ ☆ ☆ ☆
Overall Rating	☆ ☆ ☆ ☆ ☆

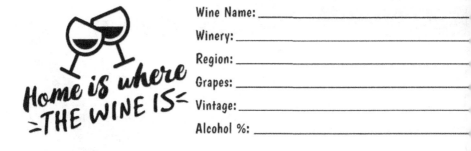

Home is where THE WINE IS

Wine Name: _____

Winery: _____

Region: _____

Grapes: _____

Vintage: _____

Alcohol %: _____

AROMA

Primary Aromas: _____

Secondary Aromas: _____

Tertiary Aromas: _____

LIFE IS TOO SHORT TO DRINK BAD WINE

TANNIN

LOW   MED   HIGH

ACIDITY

LOW   MED   HIGH

BODY

LOW   MED   HIGH

FINISH

○ Soft Finish   ○ Tart & Tingly   ○ Juicy & Fresh

WINE A BIT you'll feel better

RATING

Appearance	☆ ☆ ☆ ☆ ☆
Aroma	☆ ☆ ☆ ☆ ☆
Body	☆ ☆ ☆ ☆ ☆
Taste	☆ ☆ ☆ ☆ ☆
Finish	☆ ☆ ☆ ☆ ☆
Overall Rating	☆ ☆ ☆ ☆ ☆

time to wine down

Wine Name: _____

Winery: _____

Region: _____

Grapes: _____

Vintage: _____

Alcohol %: _____

KEEP CALM AND DRINK WINE

Wine Not?

Aroma

Primary Aromas: _____

Secondary Aromas: _____

Tertiary Aromas: _____

LOVE WINE

Finish
- ○ Soft Finish
- ○ Tart & Tingly
- ○ Juicy & Fresh

Tannin
LOW ———— MED ———— HIGH

Acidity
LOW ———— MED ———— HIGH

Body
LOW ———— MED ———— HIGH

★ Rating ★

Appearance	☆ ☆ ☆ ☆ ☆
Aroma	☆ ☆ ☆ ☆ ☆
Body	☆ ☆ ☆ ☆ ☆
Taste	☆ ☆ ☆ ☆ ☆
Finish	☆ ☆ ☆ ☆ ☆
Overall Rating	☆ ☆ ☆ ☆ ☆

Wine Name: _____

Winery: _____

Region: _____

Grapes: _____

Vintage: _____

Alcohol %: _____

Home is where =THE WINE IS=

AROMA

Primary Aromas: _____

Secondary Aromas: _____

Tertiary Aromas: _____

TANNIN
LOW   MED   HIGH

ACIDITY
LOW   MED   HIGH

BODY
LOW   MED   HIGH

FINISH

○ Soft Finish   ○ Tart & Tingly   ○ Juicy & Fresh

LIFE IS TOO SHORT TO DRINK BAD WINE

WINE A BIT *you'll feel better*

RATING		
Appearance	☆☆☆☆☆
Aroma	☆☆☆☆☆
Body	☆☆☆☆☆
Taste	☆☆☆☆☆
Finish	☆☆☆☆☆
Overall Rating	☆☆☆☆☆

Made in United States
Orlando, FL
06 June 2025

61896158R00069